Learning Japanese
Hiragana and Katakana

A Workbook for Self-Study

REVISED SECOND EDITION

Kenneth G. Henshall with **Tetsuo Takagaki**

TUTTLE Publishing

Tokyo | Rutland, Vermont | Singapore

T0027347

Published by Tuttle Publishing, an imprint of Periplus Editions (HK) Ltd.

www.tuttlepublishing.com

Copyright © 1990 by Charles E. Tuttle Publishing Company, Inc.

LCC Card No. 90-70374

ISBN: 978-1-4629-0181-4 (ebook)

Revised second edition. Previously published in 2005 as *A Guide to Learning Hiragana & Katakana* ISBN 978-0-8048-3391-2

ISBN: 978-4-8053-1227-8

Distributed by:

North America, Latin America & Europe
Tuttle Publishing
364 Innovation Drive
North Clarendon
VT 05759-9436, USA
Tel: 1 (802) 773 8930
Fax: 1 (802) 773 6993
info@tuttlepublishing.com
www.tuttlepublishing.com

Japan
Tuttle Publishing
Yaekari Building 3rd Floor
5-4-12 Osaki Shinagawa-ku
Tokyo 1410032, Japan
Tel: (81) 3 5437 0171
Fax: (81) 3 5437 0755
sales@tuttle.co.jp
www.tuttle.co.jp

"Books to Span the East and West"

Tuttle Publishing was founded in 1832 in the small New England town of Rutland, Vermont [USA]. Our core values remain as strong today as they were then—to publish best-in-class books which bring people together one page at a time. In 1948, we established a publishing office in Japan—and Tuttle is now a leader in publishing English-language books about the arts, languages and cultures of Asia. The world has become a much smaller place today and Asia's economic and cultural influence has grown. Yet the need for meaningful dialogue and information about this diverse region has never been greater. Over the past seven decades, Tuttle has published thousands of books on subjects ranging from martial arts and paper crafts to language learning and literature—and our talented authors, illustrators, designers and photographers have won many prestigious awards. We welcome you to explore the wealth of information available on Asia at www.tuttlepublishing.com.

Asia Pacific
Berkeley Books Pte Ltd
3 Kallang Sector #04-01
Singapore 349278
Tel: (65) 6741-2178
Fax: (65) 6741-2179
inquiries@periplus.com.sg
www.tuttlepublishing.com

25 24 23 22 21
18 17 16 15 14   2103VP

Printed in Malaysia

CONTENTS

PART II: **Katakana**

PART III: **Final Review**

HOW TO USE THIS BOOK

The main aim of this book is to help students achieve competence in reading and writing *kana*, the phonetic symbols that are fundamental to written Japanese. The book starts with a section entitled "An Explanation of *Kana*", which contains everything the student will need to know about the two *kana* systems of *hiragana* and *katakana*. Part I of the workbook section then systematically introduces each *hiragana* symbol, voiced form, and combination, and provides ample practice and review. Part II does the same for *katakana*, while Part III provides an overall review.

The "Explanation of *Kana*" outlines the function and origin of *kana*, the difference between the two *kana* systems, the various sounds, the combinations, and the conventions of usage. It attempts to be detailed and thorough so that it can be used for reference at any stage. Though all the information about *kana* is grouped together in this one section for ease of reference, it is not expected that the student will read it all before starting on the practice pages. In fact, to do so might give the impression that *kana* are perhaps rather formidable, which is not really the case at all. (Just ask any Japanese child!) We recommend that the student start work on the *hiragana* practice pages after reading the first three subsections on the function, origin, and basic sounds of *kana*. After finishing practice of the forty-six basic *hiragana* symbols the student should go back to the "Explanation" and read the subsection on additional sounds, then work through the rest of the *hiragana* practice pages before moving on to the *katakana* practice. The final subsection, on other points to note, is mostly concerned with special *katakana* combinations and can be left until the appropriate point in the *katakana* practice pages, just prior to the final review. Students may modify this order, but we recommend finishing practice of one *kana* system before moving on to the next.

In the practice pages of Parts I and II each *kana* symbol is allotted half a page, permitting plenty of writing practice in the boxes given. We suggest working in pencil, rather than ink, as this will allow for erasing and repeated use. Stroke order and pronunciation information are also given for each symbol and audio pronunciation files are available on the Tuttle website (see page 6). In addition, for each symbol there is an illustration of its graphic evolution from its "parent" character (see "Explanation of *Kana*") and a reference number for that character as it occurs in *A Guide to Remembering Japanese Characters* (Tuttle, 1988). This may be of interest to readers wishing to continue their studies of written Japanese to an advanced level. (However, some of the original characters are no longer commonly used and therefore are not included in *A Guide to Remembering Japanese Characters*.)

After approximately every ten symbols there are "mini review" pages for further practice, this time using whole words. These are cumulative, containing symbols not only from the group just completed but from earlier groups. The mini reviews can be used purely for copying practice, or, by covering the cue *kana* on the left side of the page, as more challenging writing exercises. They can also be used as vocabulary exercises.

Part III, the Final Review, contains exercises, quizzes, and "do-it-yourself" charts. Unlike the reviews in the first two parts it combines the two *kana* systems, as is natural in Japanese texts. And for a more natural effect the boxes used earlier in the book to help achieve even spacing and proper stroke lengths are dispensed with in this final part.

The words appearing in the reviews have been carefully chosen in keeping with an additional aim of this book, which is to expose readers to key words related to Japanese society and culture. The prime criterion for selecting review words was their suitability for practicing the *kana* symbols, but we thought it would be helpful to students if in addition these words could, whenever possible, have particular relevance to Japanese culture. About half of the 450 or so vocabulary items in the book fall into this category. It is beyond the scope of the book to explain these in detail, but students who take the trouble to find out more about them will be rewarded with a broadened appreciation of Japan's society and culture. In short, we intend that these words should be used as a sort of checklist for an exploration of Japan, rather than simply memorized as isolated vocabulary items.

Readers will occasionally encounter a semicolon between English equivalents given for a Japanese review word. This indicates that the Japanese word is a homophone, that is, a word having a different meaning but the same sound as another. Normally these homophones would be written with different characters, but when expressed in phonetic *kana* script or romanization such differentiation is not possible. The English words separated by a semicolon thus refer to different Japanese words sharing the same *kana* form. (Commas between English words simply indicate nuances of the same word.) It should also be noted that there is sometimes a subtle difference in intonation between "homophones," which cannot be determined from the *kana* or romanization.

Finally, to assist readers with the correct pronunciation of the *kana* syllables, vocabulary words, and model sentences introduced in this book, a set of audio files recorded by a native Japanese speaker is available free of charge on the Tuttle website. For each page that is marked in the book with a headset symbol (🎧), you will find the corresponding audio file at www.tuttlepublishing.com. Note that as *hiragana* and *katakana* syllables have the same pronunciation, audio files for individual syllable pronunciation are only included for the *hiragana* section of the book.

AN EXPLANATION OF *KANA*

The Function of *Kana*

Kana are purely phonetic symbols. That is, they are written representations of pronunciation. They can express the entire Japanese language in writing, though in practice the written language uses a mixture of *kana* and *kanji* (characters taken from Chinese).

There are two *kana* systems: *katakana* and *hiragana*. *Katakana* is now mainly used for words taken from languages other than Chinese. *Hiragana* is the more important of the two systems, and is used for everything not written in *katakana* or *kanji*. *Kanji* show meanings of words, though they also have pronunciations. Normally they are used for nouns and the unchanging part (the stem) of verbs, adjectives, and adverbs, while *hiragana* symbols are used for the changing parts (notably endings). For example, the verb *iku* means "go," while *ikanai* means "not go." The stem is *i-*, and this is usually written with a *kanji*, while the variable endings *-ku* and *-kanai* are written in *hiragana*. *Hiragana* is also used to write particles, and other words where *kanji* are not appropriate. To all intents and purposes the two *kana* systems are not interchangeable, and are rarely mixed within a given word. The rule is: **katakana for non-Chinese loan words, hiragana and kanji for the rest**.

The student of Japanese should ideally aim to learn all the two thousand *kanji* in common use. They play a very practical role in graphically and distinctively conveying the meaning of a written statement, unlike a purely phonetic script, and thereby aid rapid understanding. And naturally, no one can expect to read unedited Japanese texts without a knowledge of *kanji*. However, learning the *kanji* is a time-consuming task. Many of them are structurally complex, and many have a wide range of meanings and pronunciations.

Kana, on the other hand, are much fewer in number, with only forty-six basic symbols in each of the two systems. They are simple to write, and, with very few exceptions, they have fixed pronunciations. If you don't know the *kanji* for a particular word, but know the pronunciation, you can just express that entire word in *kana* (*hiragana*, that is; remember that *katakana* is for non-Chinese foreign words). In other words, while not ideal, **kana (hiragana) can substitute for kanji**. This means that even beginners can express themselves in functional written Japanese with relatively little effort.

The Origin of *Kana*

The word *kana* derives from *karina*, meaning "borrowed name," for the *kana* symbols are simplified forms of certain borrowed Chinese characters used for their sound (though, confusingly, the same characters lent their meaning in other contexts). The prefix *hira-* means "ordinary," with connotations of "informal" and "easy," and in this particular case "cursive." Thus *hiragana* means "ordinary (cursive) *kana*," and indeed *hiragana* has traditionally been the more commonly used of the two systems, and the more cursive. The *hiragana* symbols are simplifications of whole Chinese characters. For example, the *kana* あ (pronounced like the "a" in "car") derives from a cursive rendition of the character 安 (pronounced "an"). *Kata-* means "one side" or "partial," pointing to the fact that *katakana* symbols derive from one part of a Chinese character. For example, イ (pronounced like "ee" in "meet") is the left-hand part of the character 伊 (also pronounced "ee").

Both systems evolved around the end of the eighth century. In those early days *hiragana* was used mostly by women, while men preferred to use the more angular *katakana*. However, these associations have long since disappeared.

The Basic Sounds Represented by *Kana*

Kana symbols basically represent syllables, and the *kana* systems are therefore syllabaries rather than alphabets. Generally the syllables are crisp and clear combinations of one consonant and one following vowel, or one vowel by itself. There is only one consonant that exists as a syllable and *kana* symbol in its own right, *n*.

The use of English letters to refer to Japanese sounds and symbols can produce a number of apparent irregularities. Among other things a combination of consonant and vowel in Japanese will not necessarily have the same pronunciation as in English. For example, while ふ is found in the *h* group (see the table that follows), its pronunciation is actually closer to the English sound "fu" than "hu." To facilitate pronunciation the romanization used in this book is a version of the Hepburn system, which transcribes ふ as *fu* rather than *hu*, but readers should appreciate that there is no direct equivalent in Japanese to an English "f." Similar cases of convenient but seemingly irregular romanization are found in the *s* group and *t* group. This may begin to seem complicated, but in fact correspondence in Japanese between *kana* spelling and pronunciation is much simpler than in the case of English and its alphabet. Attempts to express certain loan words in *katakana* can seem awkward, but that is really a problem relating to the Japanization of non-Japanese words, rather than to the *kana* system itself.

Each of the two *kana* systems contains the same basic forty-six syllables, arranged in the same order. The basic syllabaries are as follows (combined for convenience, with the *katakana* written slightly smaller).

VOWELS

CONSONANTS		a		i		u		e		o	
		あ	ア *a*	い	イ *i*	う	ウ *u*	え	エ *e*	お	オ *o*
k		か	カ *ka*	き	キ *ki*	く	ク *ku*	け	ケ *ke*	こ	コ *ko*
s		さ	サ *sa*	し	シ *shi*	す	ス *su*	せ	セ *se*	そ	ソ *so*
t		た	タ *ta*	ち	チ *chi*	つ	ツ *tsu*	て	テ *te*	と	ト *to*
n		な	ナ *na*	に	ニ *ni*	ぬ	ヌ *nu*	ね	ネ *ne*	の	ノ *no*
h		は	ハ *ha*	ひ	ヒ *hi*	ふ	フ *fu*	へ	ヘ *he*	ほ	ホ *ho*
m		ま	マ *ma*	み	ミ *mi*	む	ム *mu*	め	メ *me*	も	モ *mo*
y		や	ヤ *ya*			ゆ	ユ *yu*			よ	ヨ *yo*
r		ら	ラ *ra*	り	リ *ri*	る	ル *ru*	れ	レ *re*	ろ	ロ *ro*
w		わ	ワ *wa*							を	ヲ *o*
n		ん	ン *n*								

This order is known as the *gojūonjun*, meaning "the fifty sounds order." In fact, there are now only forty-six basic symbols (sounds) officially in use. *Yi*, *ye*, and *wu* do not exist. *Wi* (ゐ/ヰ) and *we* (ゑ/ヱ) were officially removed from the list in 1946 since the sounds were considered sufficiently close to *i* and *e* to be represented by the symbols for these. However, the symbols for *wi* and *we* are still encountered on rare occasions.

The *gojūonjun* is the standard order followed by dictionaries and other reference works. It is therefore particularly important to remember it. To this end the following mnemonic, which is a modified version of one taught by Professors Dunn and O'Neill of the University of London, may be helpful:

Ah, *kana* signs! Take note how many you read well (n).

The first letters of these words follow the *gojūonjun* consonant headings. With apologies to mathematicians, even the syllable *n* (ん) is represented, by the mathematical symbol *n* indicating the utmost number (in this case ninety-two, the sum of the two *kana* systems).

The syllable *n* (ん) is sometimes called the "independent *n*" but it can never be used truly independently. Nor can it ever start a word. When working from romanization it is sometimes difficult to tell whether a non-initial *n* followed by a vowel is a syllable from the *n-* group, or whether it is *n* (ん) followed by an independent vowel. For example, *tani* could be either たに (valley) or たんい (unit). Context usually makes this clear. To avoid ambiguity some romanization systems use an apostrophe after the *n* that represents ん. Thus たんい can be romanized as *tan'i*. Note also that in romanization ん is sometimes written as *m* before a *p*, *b*, or *m*, as in *shimbun* for *shinbun* (newspaper). This practice is by no means universally followed (and is not followed in this book), but its existence does indicate one of the exceptional cases where the pronunciation of a *kana* symbol could be said to vary slightly according to context.

Additional Sounds Represented by *Kana*

In addition to the forty-six basic symbols, there are sixty-one classified modifications and combinations in each system, and a few further special combinations as well. This may sound alarming, but in fact it involves only a handful of new points to learn.

VOWELS

CONSONANTS		*a*		*i*		*u*		*e*		*o*	
g	が	ガ / ga	ぎ	ギ / gi	ぐ	グ / gu	げ	ゲ / ge	ご	ゴ / go
z/j	ざ	ザ / za	じ	ジ / ji	ず	ズ / zu	ぜ	ゼ / ze	ぞ	ゾ / zo
d/z/j	だ	ダ / da	ぢ	ヂ / ji	づ	ヅ / zu	で	デ / de	ど	ド / do
b	ば	バ / ba	び	ビ / bi	ぶ	ブ / bu	べ	ベ / be	ぼ	ボ / bo
p	ぱ	パ / pa	ぴ	ピ / pi	ぷ	プ / pu	ぺ	ペ / pe	ぽ	ポ / po

The first is the *dakuon*, meaning "voiced sound" or "hardened sound." Sounds starting with the unvoiced consonants *k*, *s*, *t*, and *h* are voiced as *g*, *z/j*, *d/z/j*, and *b* respectively if the diacritical marks ` are added to the upper right side of the basic *kana* symbol, as shown in the following table. (See also pp. 49–53.) The table also shows *handakuon*, meaning "half-voiced sound," which applies only to sounds starting with *h*. The addition of a small circle ° to the upper right side of the appropriate basic *kana* symbol changes the pronunciation from *h* to *p* (as opposed to changing it to *b* in the case of the full *dakuon*).

Ji and *zu* are written じ and ず, except when they clearly derive from *chi* (ち) and *tsu* (つ) in compounds or repeated symbols. For example, *hanaji* (nosebleed, from *hana* [nose] and *chi* [blood]) is はなぢ, and *tsuzuku* (continue, from *tsutsuku*) is つづく.

A combination of a consonant and *y-* is known as a *yōon*, meaning "contracted sound." Any of the seven basic consonants *k*, *s*, *t*, *n*, *h*, *m*, or *r*, or voiced or half-voiced consonants, can be used. The symbol that represents these consonants plus *i*, for example き (*ki*) or し (*shi*), is followed by a symbol from the *y-* group—either *ya*, *yu*, or *yo* as appropriate. This second symbol is written smaller, while the *i* sound is barely pronounced and is dropped in romanization. Thus *kyo* is expressed as きょ and *shu* (*syu* in some romanization systems) as しゅ. If the ょ or ゅ of our examples were written the same size as the preceding symbols, then they would be treated as uncombined symbols and read *kiyo* or *shiyu* respectively. Full tables are given below. (See also pp. 56–59.)

	a		*u*		*o*	
ky	きゃ	キャ *kya*	きゅ	キュ *kyu*	きょ	キョ *kyo*
sh	しゃ	シャ *sha*	しゅ	シュ *shu*	しょ	ショ *sho*
ch	ちゃ	チャ *cha*	ちゅ	チュ *chu*	ちょ	チョ *cho*
ny	にゃ	ニャ *nya*	にゅ	ニュ *nyu*	にょ	ニョ *nyo*
hy	ひゃ	ヒャ *hya*	ひゅ	ヒュ *hyu*	ひょ	ヒョ *hyo*
my	みゃ	ミャ *mya*	みゅ	ミュ *myu*	みょ	ミョ *myo*
ry	りゃ	リャ *rya*	りゅ	リュ *ryu*	りょ	リョ *ryo*

	a		*u*		*o*	
gy	ぎゃ	ギャ *gya*	ぎゅ	ギュ *gyu*	ぎょ	ギョ *gyo*
j	じゃ	ジャ *ja*	じゅ	ジュ *ju*	じょ	ジョ *jo*
j	ぢゃ	ヂャ *ja*	ぢゅ	ヂュ *ju*	ぢょ	ヂョ *jo*
by	びゃ	ビャ *bya*	びゅ	ビュ *byu*	びょ	ビョ *byo*
py	ぴゃ	ピャ *pya*	ぴゅ	ピュ *pyu*	ぴょ	ピョ *pyo*

Note that ヂ combinations rarely occur.

Some consonants—essentially *k, s, t,* and *p*—can be doubled by inserting a small *tsu* (っ or ッ) in front of them. This combination is known as a *sokuon* (double consonant). Thus *gakki* (school term) is expressed as がっき. The little っ or ッ is not pronounced as such, but the consonant that follows it is given, as it were, a double amount of time for its pronunciation. It is important to apply this extra time to the consonant only, and not to the following vowel. Thus the word in our example should be pronounced *gakki* and not *gakkii*. These double consonants can never begin a word. (See also pp. 54–55.)

Students commonly make the mistake of trying to write a double *n*, as in words like *annai* (guide), with a small っ. The correct way is to use ん to represent the first *n*. Thus *annai* should be written あんない.

The lengthening of vowels (including the vowel sound of syllables in which a consonant precedes the vowel) can also cause errors, especially in the case of the long *o*. In romanization long vowels are usually indicated (if at all) either by writing the vowel twice or by a macron, as in *uu* or *ū* for a long *u*. For loan words in *katakana*, a barlike symbol ー (or | with vertical script) is used. Thus *rabā* (rubber) is written ラバー. In *hiragana*, the vowels *a, i, u,* and *e* are doubled by simply writing あ, い, う, or え respectively after the preceding symbol. Thus *okāsan* (mother) is written おかあさん. (The doubling of *a* and *e* actually occurs infrequently in *hiragana*. What sounds like a long *e* is usually *e* followed by *i*, as in せんせい, *sensei* [teacher].) A long *o* can sometimes be formed by doubling in the same way as with other vowels, that is, by adding お (*o*) but it is more commonly formed by adding う (*u*). Thus *sō* (so, thus) is written そう. The long *o* that takes お was once pronounced slightly differently from the long *o* that takes う, but that is no longer true, and it is necessary to learn each word with a long *o* sound case by case. Fortunately, there are only a few common words that require the addition of お as opposed to う. These include *ōkii* (big, おおきい), *ōi* (many, おおい),

tōi (far, とおい), *tō* (ten, とお), and *tōri* (way, road, とおり). Students should take particular care not to be misled by the common romanization practice of writing a long *o* as *oo*, when in *hiragana* it is usually お (*o*) plus う (*u*).

Caution is also needed when transcribing from *kana* to romanization. Always check that an apparent long vowel really is a long vowel, and not two unlinked vowels, A typical case of the latter is a verb whose variable ending starts with the same vowel as the last vowel of the stem, or appears to combine with it to make a long *o*. For example, the verb そう, meaning "go with," should always be romanized as *sou* and not *sō* or *soo*. (By contrast, そう meaning "thus," being a genuine long vowel, is romanized as *sō* or *soo*.) Similarly, *suu* is the romanization for the verb すう (suck), rather than *sū*, and *kiite* is the way to romanize the suspensive きいて (listening), rather than *kīte*.

Other Points to Note

There are three common cases where *kana* usage is distinctly irregular. They all involve particles, namely the topic particle *wa*, the object particle *o*, and the directional particle *e* (meaning "to"). These words are written は, を, and へ respectively, and not わ, お, and え as might be expected. The irregularities result from the failure of writing conventions to keep pace with pronunciation changes over the last century or so.

Certain further usages need to be noted with regard to *katakana* loan words only. These are relatively recent attempts to express non-Japanese words with greater accuracy, and tend to be an extension of the *yōon* principle (きょ etc.) described on page 11. That is, they combine two *kana* symbols, the first one lending only its consonant sound and this fact being indicated by the small size of the second symbol. For example, "f" sounds can be approximated by following *fu* (フ) with a small vowel. Thus *fa, fi, fe*, and *fo* are written as ファ, フィ, フェ, and フォ respectively. Similarly, "q" can be represented by *ku* (ク) plus a small vowel, as in クォーター (quarter). A German-style "z" (as in "Mozart") can be shown by *tsu* (ツ) plus a small vowel, i.e., モーツァルト (Mozart). "She" (as in "shepherd"), "che" (as in "check"), and the voiced version "je" are written as シェ, チェ, and ジェ. Though not a consonant, *u* (ウ) is used in a similar type of combination, to produce "w" sounds. As mentioned earlier, the sounds *wi* and *we* are still occasionally found expressed by ヰ and ヱ respectively, but nowadays are usually written as ウィ and ウェ Thus "whisky" (*uisukī*) is usually written as ウィスキー. Theoretically ヲ could be used for *wo*, but this has become so associated with the object particle *o* that ウォ is used instead. (*Wa*, however, is represented by ワ.) In similar fashion, *i* (イ) can be followed by a small エ to express "ye." Thus "Yemen" is イェーメン. Remarkably, an extension of the use of ウ has seen diacritical marks added to it in order to express "v." Thus "Venus" is ヴィーナス. The English sounds "ty" or "ti" (as in "party") and their voiced equivalents "dy" and "di," which were once expressed rather unfaithfully by チ and ジ respectively, are now written as ティ and ディ. Thus "party" is パーティー. The "tu" of "tuba" and the "du" of "due" can be expressed by テュ and デュ, giving テューバ

(tuba) and デュエット (duet), while the "Tou" of "Toulouse" can be shown by トゥ (a voiced version is also possible).

These combinations have received official approval, particularly when used in place names and personal names. However, there is also official recognition of established usage, such as of *b* for *v*. This means that in practice some words can be written in a number of ways. "Violin" can be either ヴァイオリン or バイオリン, for example. In cases where a certain usage has become particularly firmly entrenched in the Japanese language the old rendition is favored, such as ミルクセーキ (*mirukusēki*) for "milkshake" (but note that "Shakespeare" is シェークスピア). At the same time, it is also possible to make up new combinations as appropriate, such as ニ (*ni*) plus a small エ (*e*) to express the *nye* sound of the Russian *nyet*. In short, the student should be prepared for a range of creative and sometimes inconsistent usages.

Katakana is very occasionally used for words other than loan words. For example, it can be used to emphasize or highlight words, such as entries in academic reference works, and is also used in telegrams and certain military and official documents. In such cases, when used for purely Japanese or Chinese-derived words, its conventions of usage are identical to those of *hiragana*. Long vowels, for instance, are formed by adding the appropriate vowel and not by a bar. Thus *gakkō* (school) is ガッコウ, rather than ガッコー.

A *kana* symbol can be repeated by the special symbol ヽ. This can also be used when the second symbol is a voiced version of the first, in which case it becomes ヾ. Where more than one syllable is repeated, in vertical script only, 〱 (or 〲 if the first of the repeated sounds is voiced) can be used, with the symbol covering two spaces. These repetition symbols are known collectively as *odoriji* (jump symbols). Students need to recognize them, but should only use them, if at all, with caution. They are not compulsory, and have a number of restrictions on their usage. For example, they cannot be used where the first symbol of one word is the same as the last symbol of the word that precedes it (as in *kuroi ishi* meaning "black stone"), or similarly in compound words where the first symbol of the second word coincides with the last symbol of the first word (as in *tama-matsuri* meaning "festival of the dead"), or where the first symbol of a variable word ending is the same as the last symbol of the word stem (as in *ki-kimasu* meaning "listen"). Some examples of correct usage:

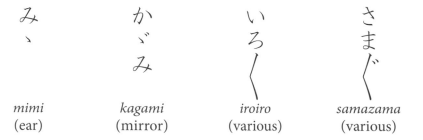

| mimi | kagami | iroiro | samazama |
| (ear) | (mirror) | (various) | (various) |

Finally, students should learn the basic Japanese punctuation marks, known as *kutōten*. Full stops are written 。 (*maru*), and commas are written 、 (*ten*). Quotation marks (*kagi*) are written 「　」 in horizontal script and in vertical script.

PART I

Hiragana

□

⬇

**The Online Audio files for pronunciation practice
may be Downloaded.**

To download the audios for this book, type the URL below
into to your web browser.

http://www.tuttlepublishing.com/learning-japanese-hiragana-
and-katakana-downloadable-cd-content

For support, email us at info@tuttlepublishing.com

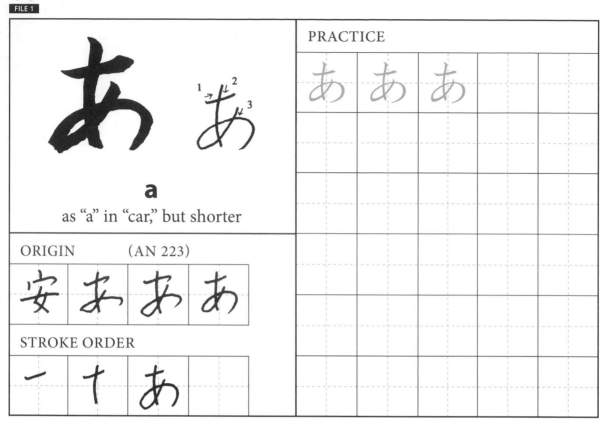

a

as "a" in "car," but shorter

ORIGIN   (AN 223)

STROKE ORDER

PRACTICE

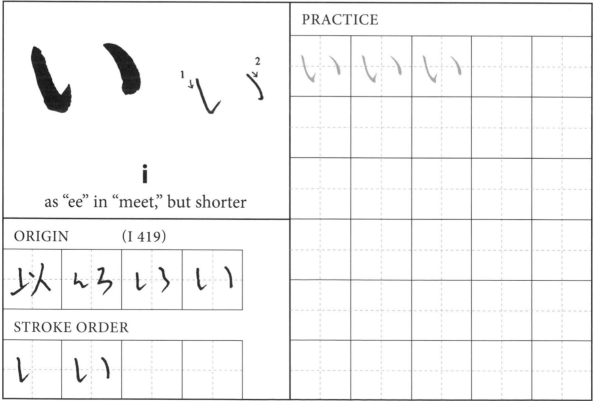

i

as "ee" in "meet," but shorter

ORIGIN   (I 419)

STROKE ORDER

PRACTICE

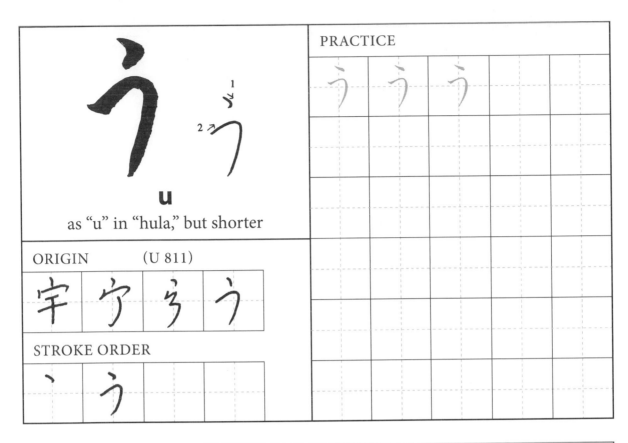

u

as "u" in "hula," but shorter

ORIGIN   (U 811)

STROKE ORDER

PRACTICE

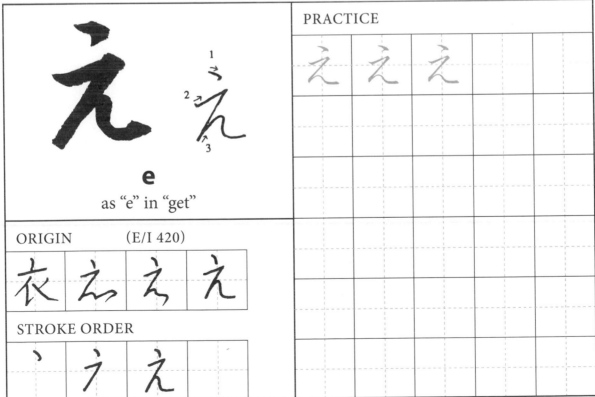

e

as "e" in "get"

ORIGIN   (E/I 420)

STROKE ORDER

PRACTICE

17

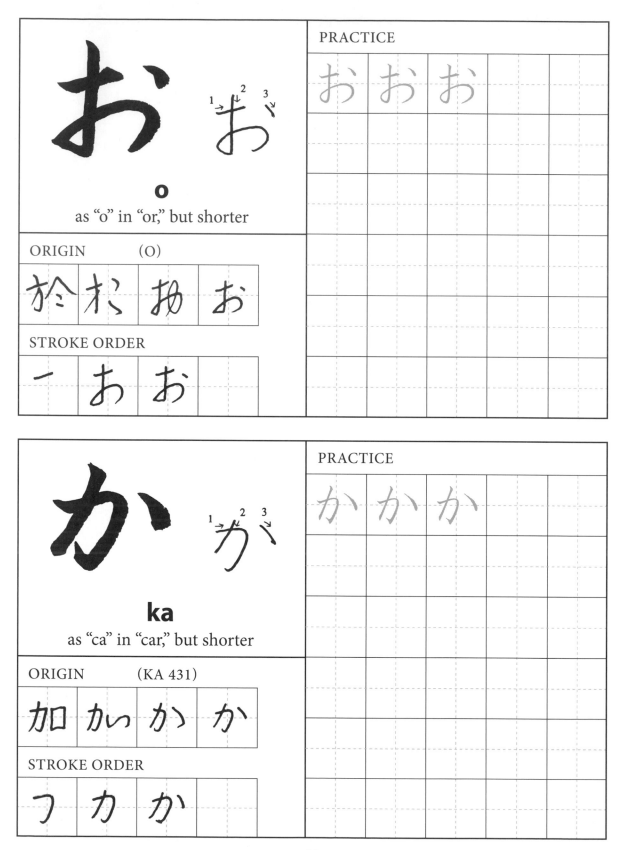

o

as "o" in "or," but shorter

ORIGIN   (O)

STROKE ORDER

PRACTICE

おおお

ka

as "ca" in "car," but shorter

ORIGIN   (KA 431)

STROKE ORDER

PRACTICE

かかか

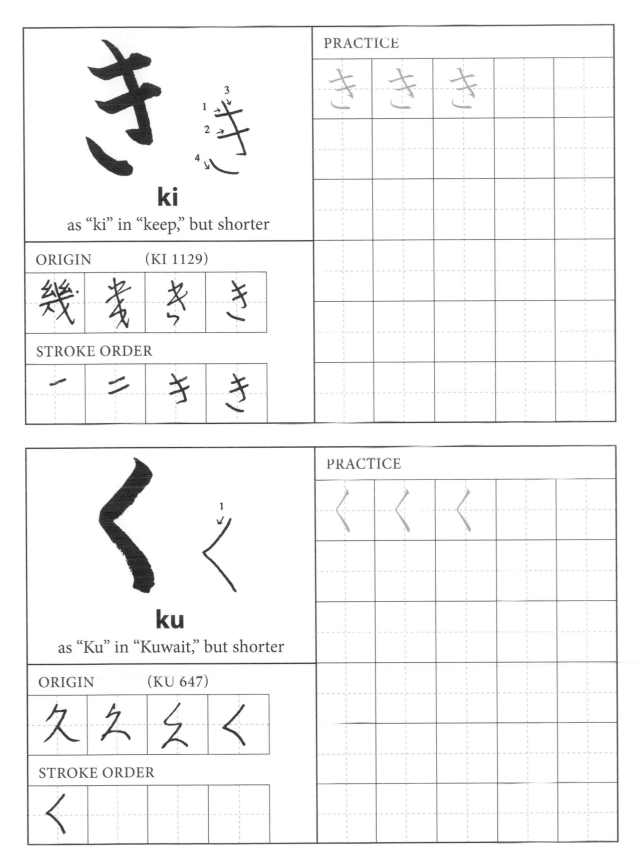

ki

as "ki" in "keep," but shorter

ORIGIN (KI 1129)

STROKE ORDER

PRACTICE

ku

as "Ku" in "Kuwait," but shorter

ORIGIN (KU 647)

STROKE ORDER

PRACTICE

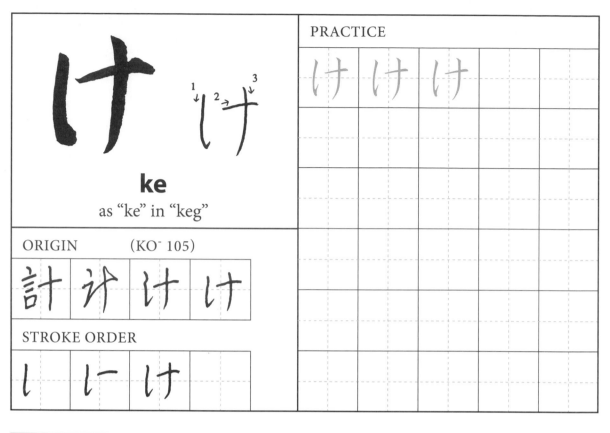

ke

as "ke" in "keg"

ORIGIN   (KO⁻ 105)

STROKE ORDER

PRACTICE

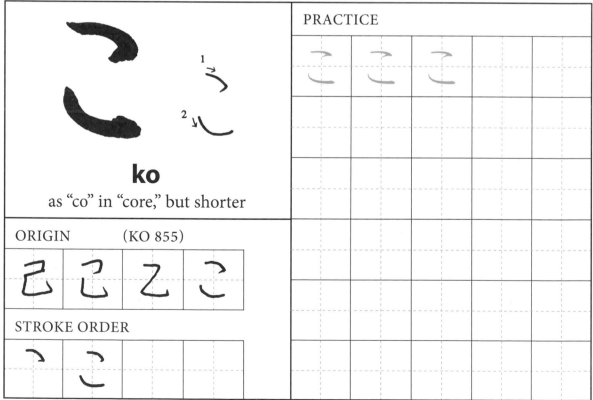

ko

as "co" in "core," but shorter

ORIGIN   (KO 855)

STROKE ORDER

PRACTICE

MINI REVIEW あ — こ / A — KO

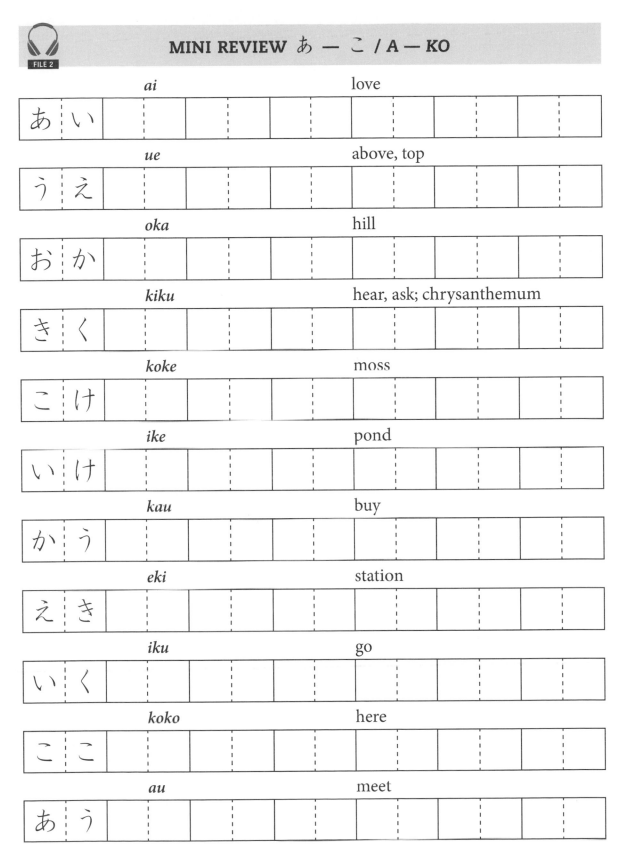

ai — love
あ い

ue — above, top
う え

oka — hill
お か

kiku — hear, ask; chrysanthemum
き く

koke — moss
こ け

ike — pond
い け

kau — buy
か う

eki — station
え き

iku — go
い く

koko — here
こ こ

au — meet
あ う

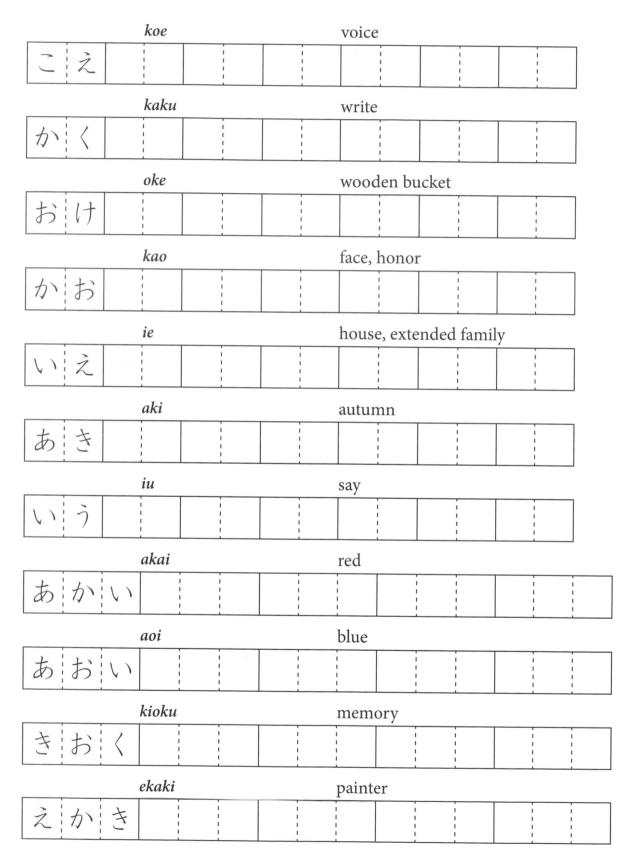

koe — voice
こ え

kaku — write
か く

oke — wooden bucket
お け

kao — face, honor
か お

ie — house, extended family
い え

aki — autumn
あ き

iu — say
い う

akai — red
あ か い

aoi — blue
あ お い

kioku — memory
き お く

ekaki — painter
え か き

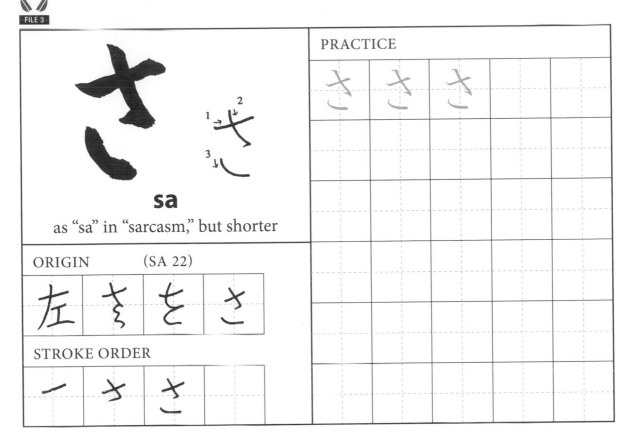

sa

as "sa" in "sarcasm," but shorter

ORIGIN   (SA 22)

左 さ を さ

STROKE ORDER

一 さ さ

PRACTICE

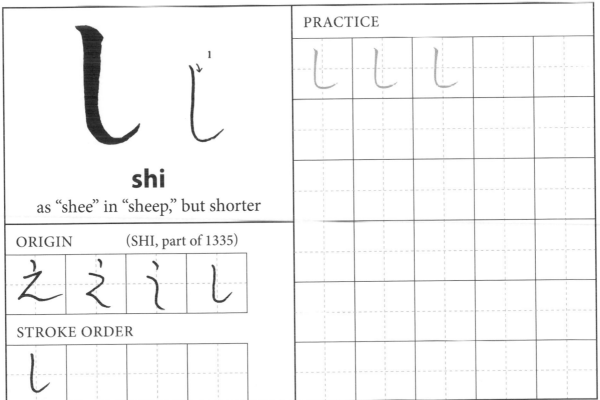

shi

as "shee" in "sheep," but shorter

ORIGIN   (SHI, part of 1335)

え え し し

STROKE ORDER

し

PRACTICE

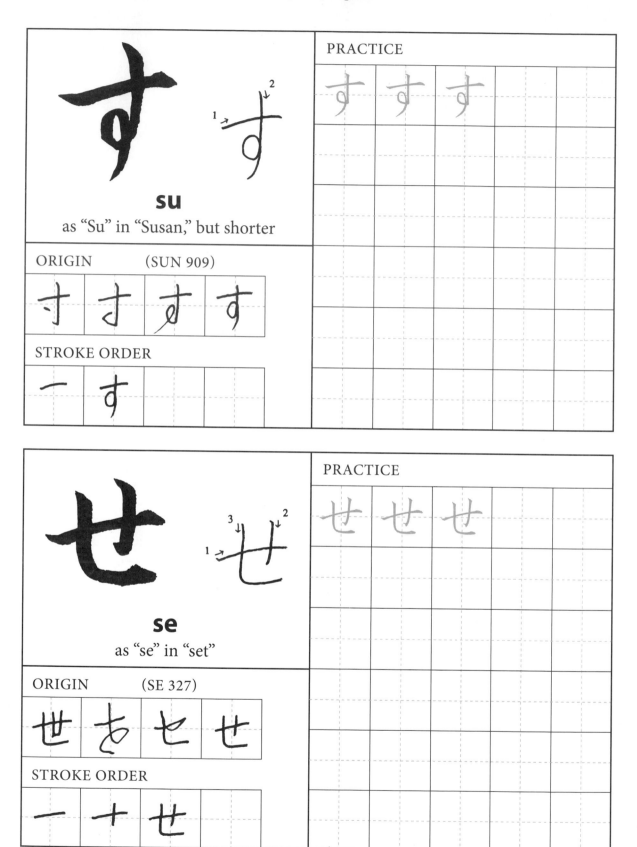

su

as "Su" in "Susan," but shorter

ORIGIN   (SUN 909)

STROKE ORDER

PRACTICE

se

as "se" in "set"

ORIGIN   (SE 327)

STROKE ORDER

PRACTICE

PRACTICE

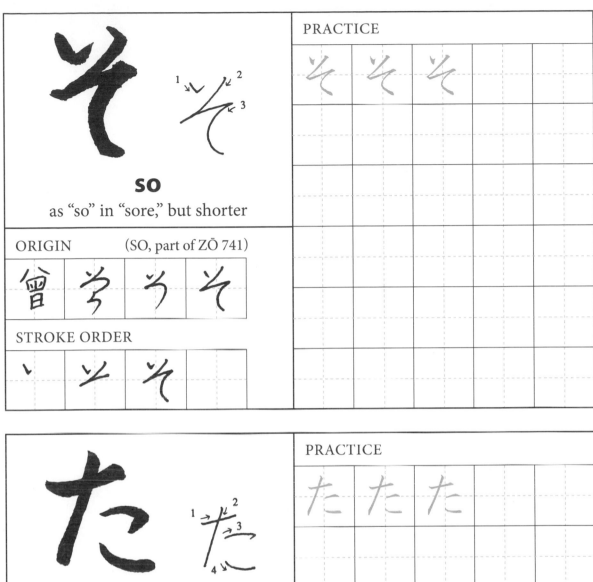

so

as "so" in "sore," but shorter

ORIGIN   (SO, part of ZŌ 741)

曾　号　ろ　そ

STROKE ORDER

丶　ヒ　そ

PRACTICE

ta

as "ta" in "tar," but shorter

ORIGIN   (TA 164)

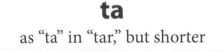
太　右　た　た

STROKE ORDER

一　十　た　た

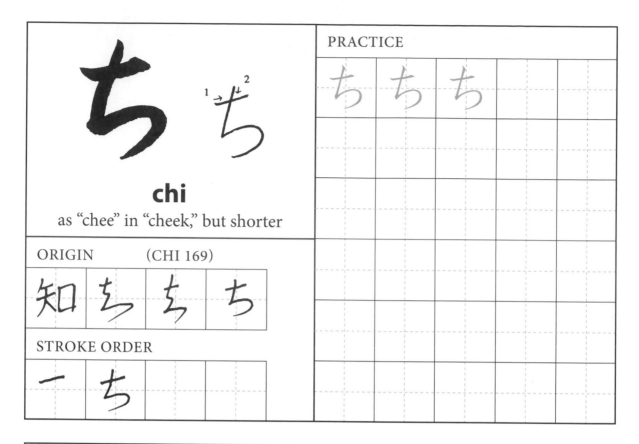

chi

as "chee" in "cheek," but shorter

ORIGIN   (CHI 169)

STROKE ORDER

tsu

as "tsu" in "tsunami"

ORIGIN   (SU 304)

STROKE ORDER

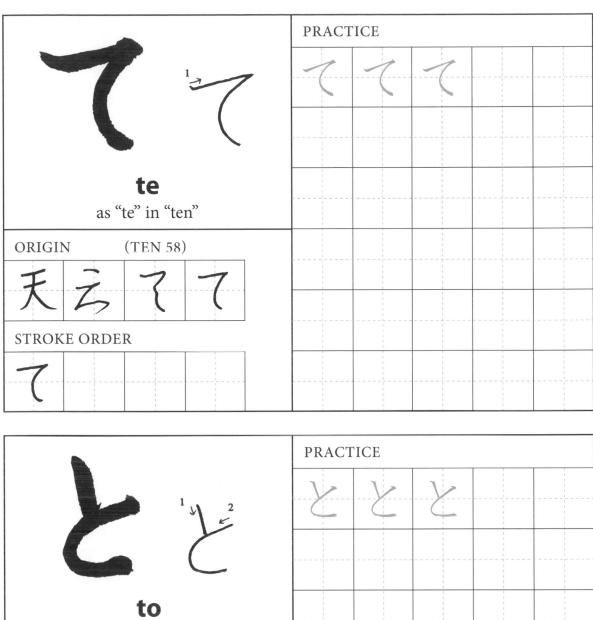

te

as "te" in "ten"

ORIGIN   (TEN 58)

STROKE ORDER

PRACTICE

to

as "to" in "tore," but shorter

ORIGIN   (TO-maru 129)

STROKE ORDER

PRACTICE

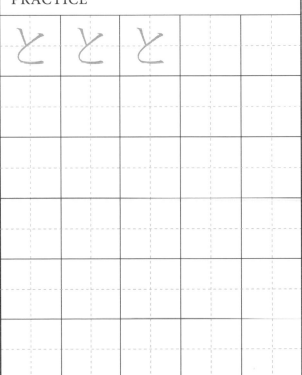

MINI REVIEW さ ─ と / SA ─ TO

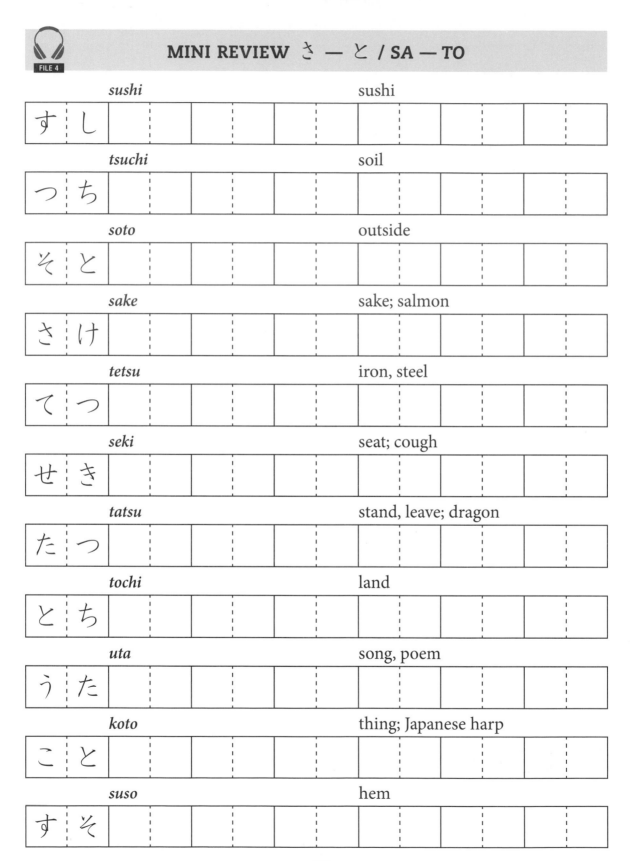

sushi   sushi

すし

tsuchi   soil

つち

soto   outside

そと

sake   sake; salmon

さけ

tetsu   iron, steel

てつ

seki   seat; cough

せき

tatsu   stand, leave; dragon

たつ

tochi   land

とち

uta   song, poem

うた

koto   thing; Japanese harp

こと

suso   hem

すそ

tai　　　　　　　sea bream

たい

teki　　　　　　enemy

てき

shichi　　　　　seven

しち

ase　　　　　　sweat

あせ

sasu　　　　　　thrust; indicate

さす

uso　　　　　　untruth

うそ

kisetsu　　　　　season

きせつ

ashita　　　　　tomorrow

あした

satoi　　　　　　clever, sharp (of senses)

さとい

sekitei　　　　　rock garden (Japanese style)

せきてい

chikatetsu　　　　subway

ちかてつ

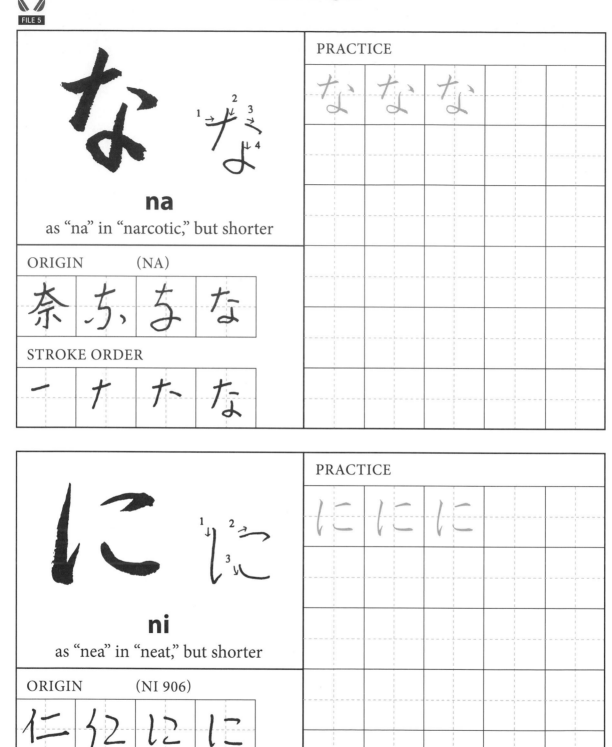

na

as "na" in "narcotic," but shorter

ORIGIN   (NA)

STROKE ORDER

PRACTICE

ni

as "nea" in "neat," but shorter

ORIGIN   (NI 906)

STROKE ORDER

PRACTICE

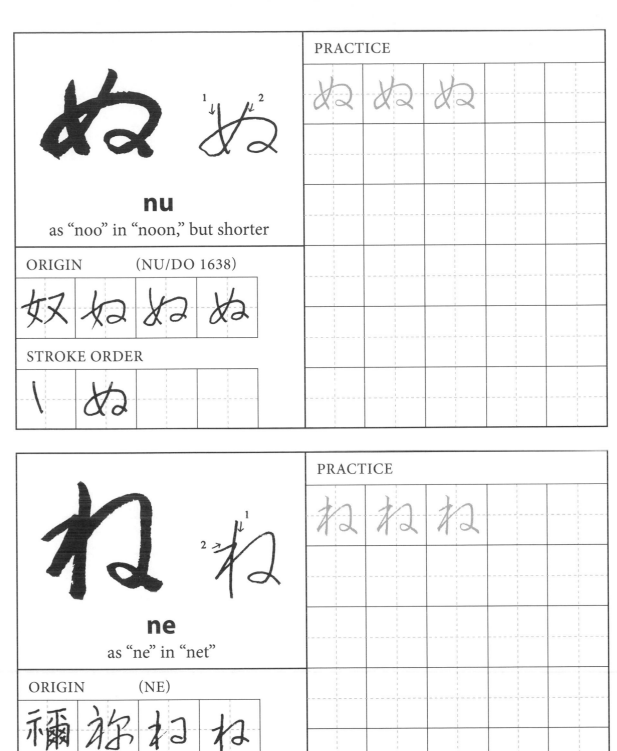

PRACTICE

nu
as "noo" in "noon," but shorter

ORIGIN   (NU/DO 1638)

STROKE ORDER

PRACTICE

ne
as "ne" in "net"

ORIGIN   (NE)

STROKE ORDER

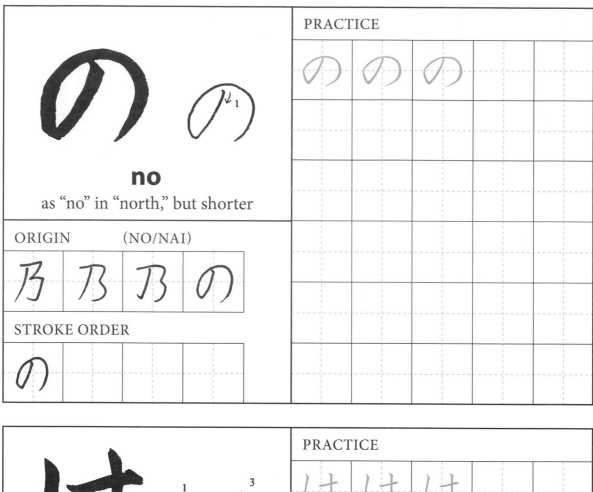

no

as "no" in "north," but shorter

ORIGIN   (NO/NAI)

STROKE ORDER

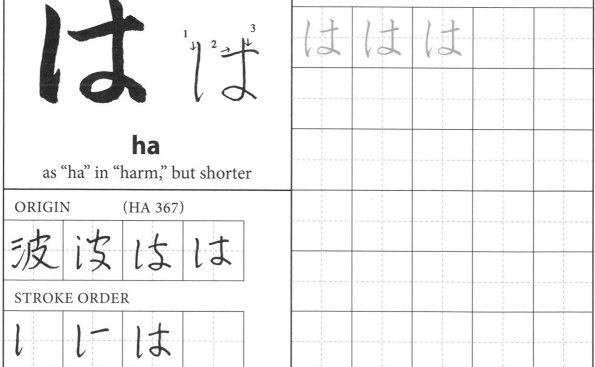

ha

as "ha" in "harm," but shorter

ORIGIN   (HA 367)

STROKE ORDER

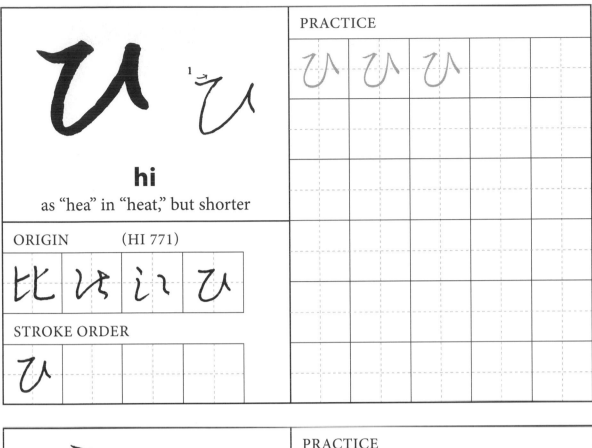

hi

as "hea" in "heat," but shorter

ORIGIN   (HI 771)

STROKE ORDER

PRACTICE

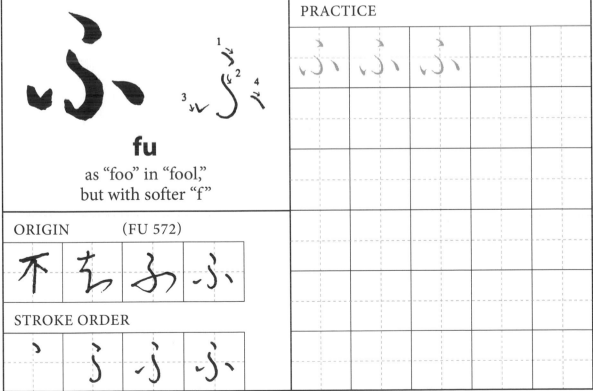

fu

as "foo" in "fool,"
but with softer "f"

ORIGIN   (FU 572)

STROKE ORDER

PRACTICE

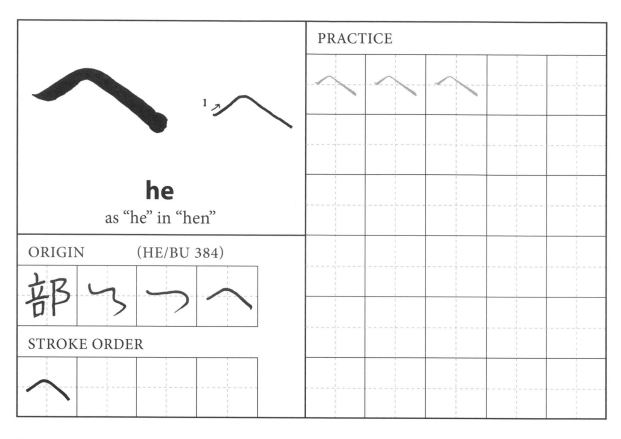

he

as "he" in "hen"

ORIGIN   (HE/BU 384)

STROKE ORDER

PRACTICE

ho

as "ho" in "horn," but shorter

ORIGIN   (HO 787)

STROKE ORDER

PRACTICE

MINI REVIEW な ー ほ / NA ー HO

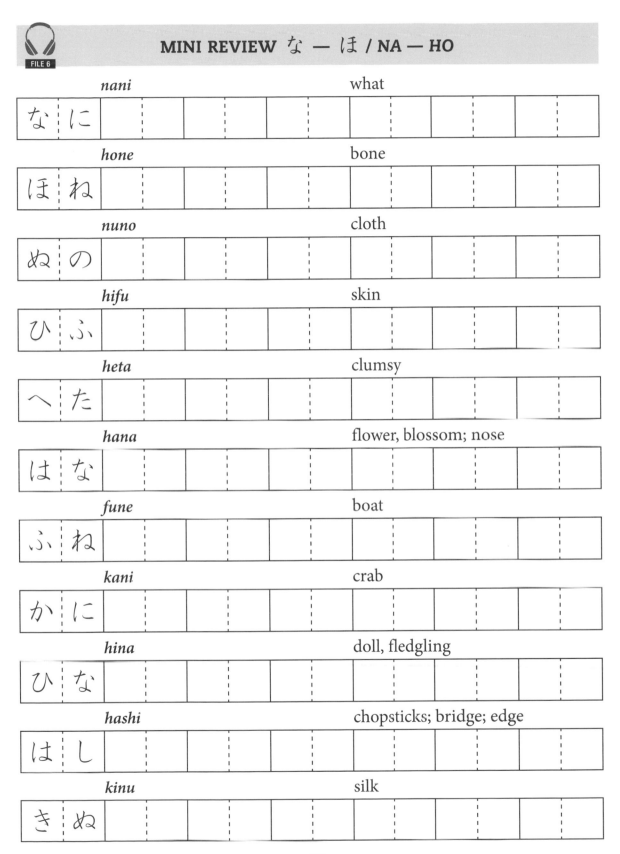

nani		what
な に		

hone		bone
ほ ね		

nuno		cloth
ぬ の		

hifu		skin
ひ ふ		

heta		clumsy
へ た		

hana		flower, blossom; nose
は な		

fune		boat
ふ ね		

kani		crab
か に		

hina		doll, fledgling
ひ な		

hashi		chopsticks; bridge; edge
は し		

kinu		silk
き ぬ		

35

hoshi   star

ほ	し						

hito   person

ひ	と						

noki   eaves

の	き						

nishi   west

に	し						

haiku   haiku

は	い	く				

katana   curved sword

か	た	な				

netsuke   carved figurine

ね	つ	け				

tanuki   raccoon dog

た	ぬ	き				

seifu   government

せ	い	ふ				

inoshishi   wild boar

い	の	し	し		

heisotsu   soldier

へ	い	そ	つ		

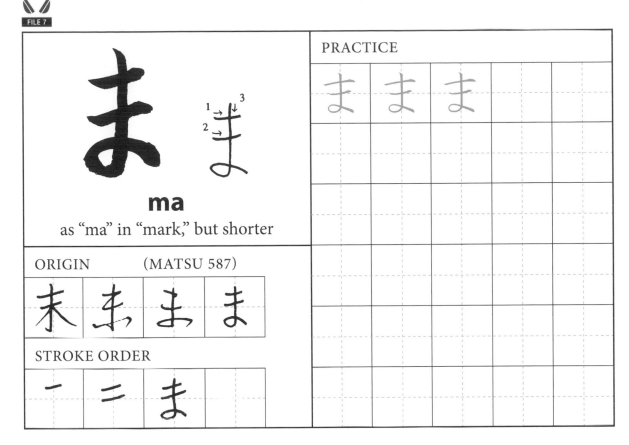

ma

as "ma" in "mark," but shorter

ORIGIN		(MATSU 587)	
末	耒	ま	ま

STROKE ORDER			
一	二	ま	

PRACTICE

mi

as "mea" in "meat," but shorter

ORIGIN		(BI 376)	
美	耂	み	み

STROKE ORDER			
み	み		

PRACTICE

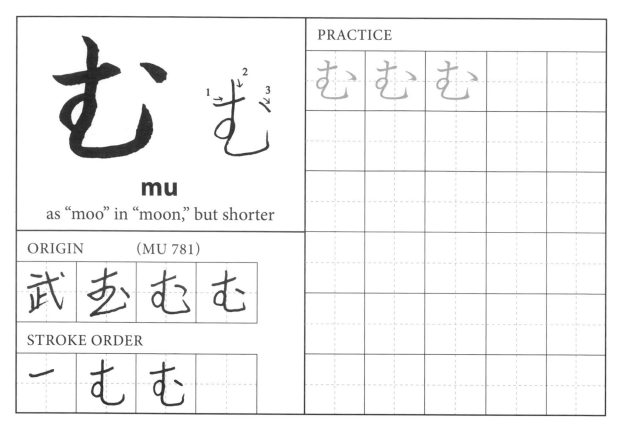

mu

as "moo" in "moon," but shorter

ORIGIN   (MU 781)

武　ざ　む　む

STROKE ORDER

一　む　む

PRACTICE

む　む　む

me

as "me" in "met"

ORIGIN   (ME 35)

女　女　め　め

STROKE ORDER

乀　め

PRACTICE

め　め　め

38

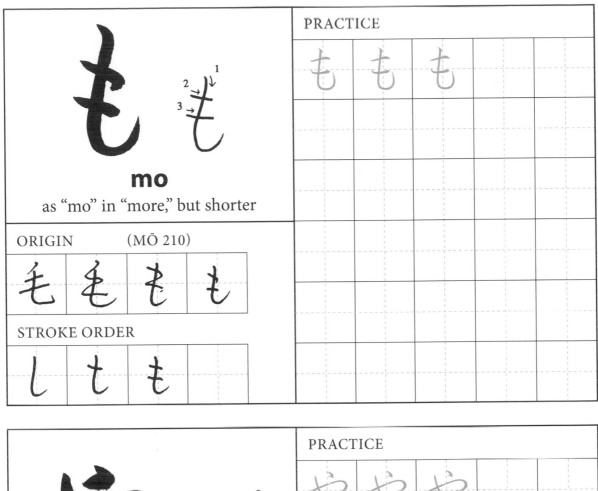

mo

as "mo" in "more," but shorter

ORIGIN   (MŌ 210)

STROKE ORDER

PRACTICE

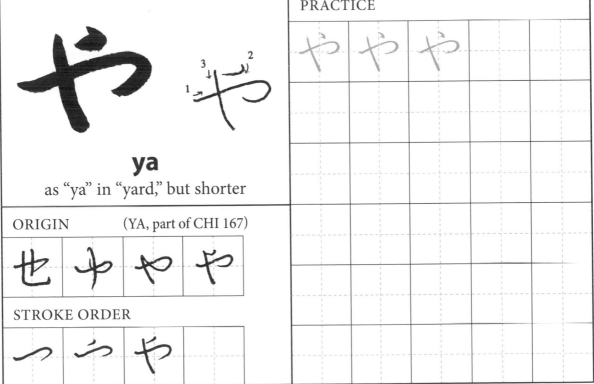

ya

as "ya" in "yard," but shorter

ORIGIN   (YA, part of CHI 167)

STROKE ORDER

PRACTICE

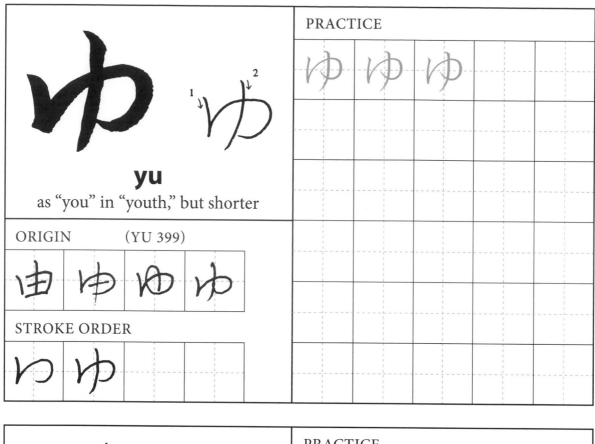

yu

as "you" in "youth," but shorter

ORIGIN   (YU 399)

STROKE ORDER

PRACTICE

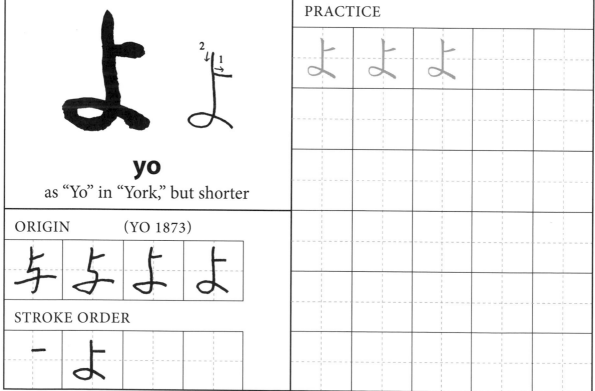

yo

as "Yo" in "York," but shorter

ORIGIN   (YO 1873)

STROKE ORDER

PRACTICE

MINI REVIEW ま ー よ / MA ー YO

FILE 8

| *yama* | | | | | | | | mountain, hill |

や　ま

| *yume* | | | | | | | | dream |

ゆ　め

| *yomu* | | | | | | | | read |

よ　む

| *momo* | | | | | | | | peach |

も　も

| *miya* | | | | | | | | shrine |

み　や

| *kome* | | | | | | | | uncooked rice |

こ　め

| *tsuyu* | | | | | | | | dew |

つ　ゆ

| *mushi* | | | | | | | | insect |

む　し

| *matsu* | | | | | | | | pine; wait |

ま　つ

| *ume* | | | | | | | | Japanese plum |

う　め

| *mune* | | | | | | | | chest, breast |

む　ね

41

kimono   kimono, clothing

き も の

sashimi   sliced raw fish

さ し み

Yamato   old name for Japan

や ま と

yukata   cotton kimono

ゆ か た

sumie   India-ink drawing

す み え

emaki   picture scroll

え ま き

hanami   blossom viewing

は な み

mikoshi   portable shrine

み こ し

ukiyoe   woodblock print

う き よ え

setomono   porcelain

せ と も の

sukiyaki   sukiyaki

す き や き

FILE 9

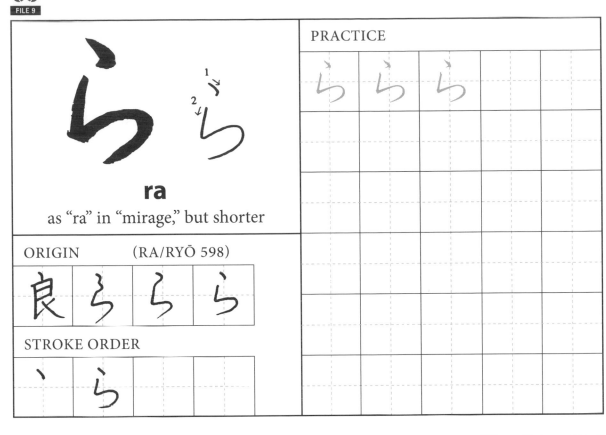

ra

as "ra" in "mirage," but shorter

ORIGIN   (RA/RYŌ 598)

STROKE ORDER

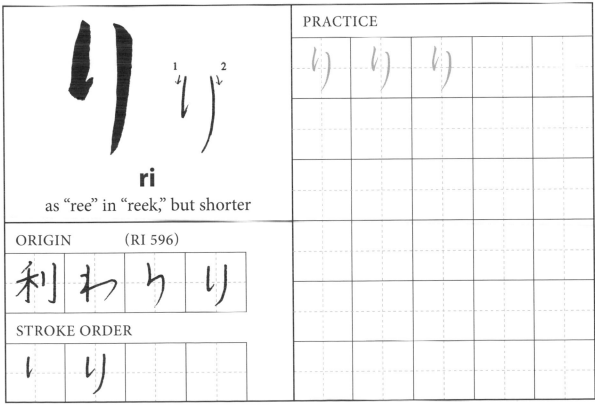

ri

as "ree" in "reek," but shorter

ORIGIN   (RI 596)

STROKE ORDER

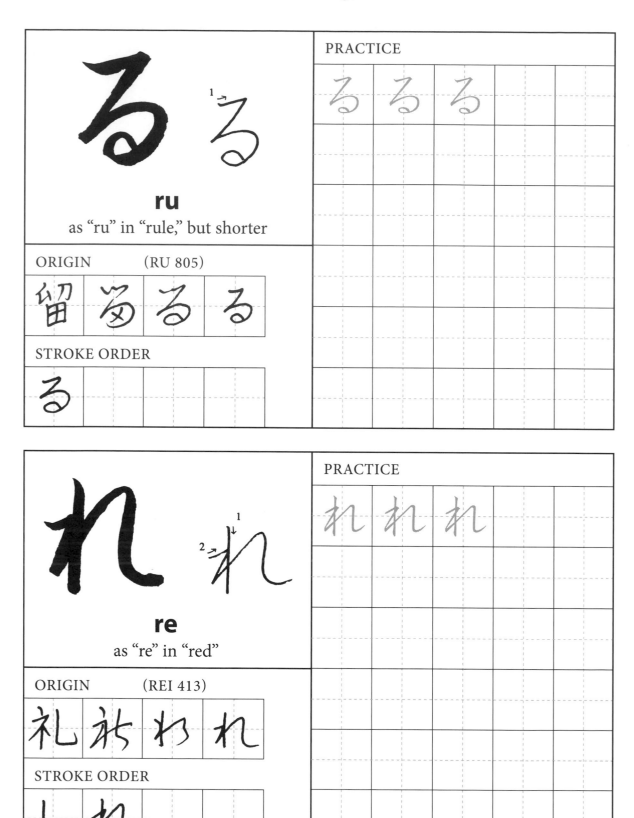

ru

as "ru" in "rule," but shorter

ORIGIN   (RU 805)

STROKE ORDER

PRACTICE

re

as "re" in "red"

ORIGIN   (REI 413)

STROKE ORDER

PRACTICE

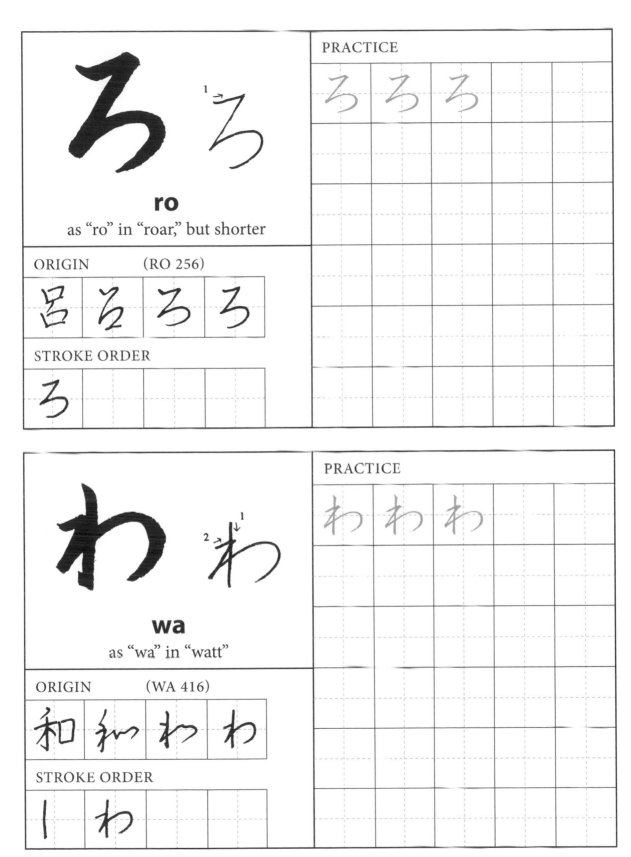

ro

as "ro" in "roar," but shorter

ORIGIN   (RO 256)

STROKE ORDER

PRACTICE

wa

as "wa" in "watt"

ORIGIN   (WA 416)

STROKE ORDER

PRACTICE

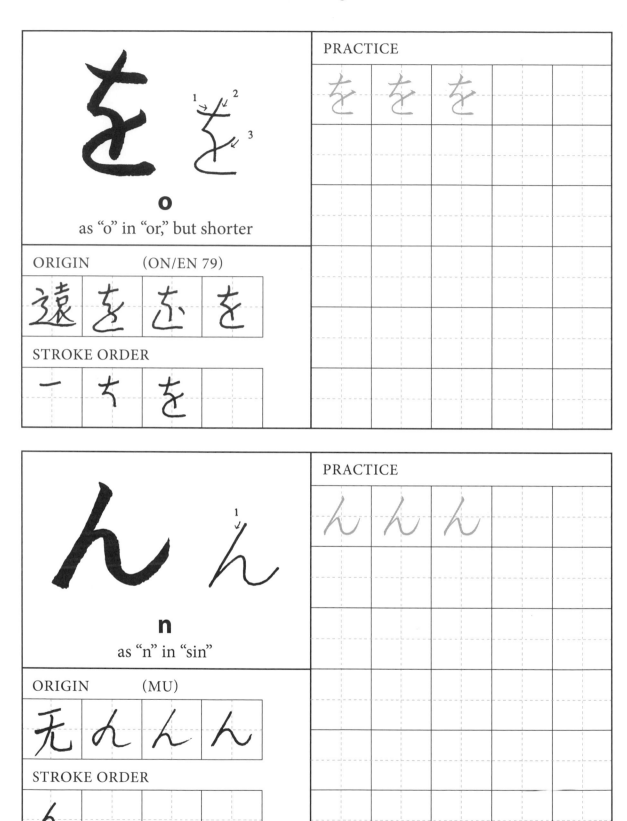

o

as "o" in "or," but shorter

ORIGIN   (ON/EN 79)

STROKE ORDER

PRACTICE

n

as "n" in "sin"

ORIGIN   (MU)

STROKE ORDER

PRACTICE

MINI REVIEW ら — ん / RA — N

FILE 10

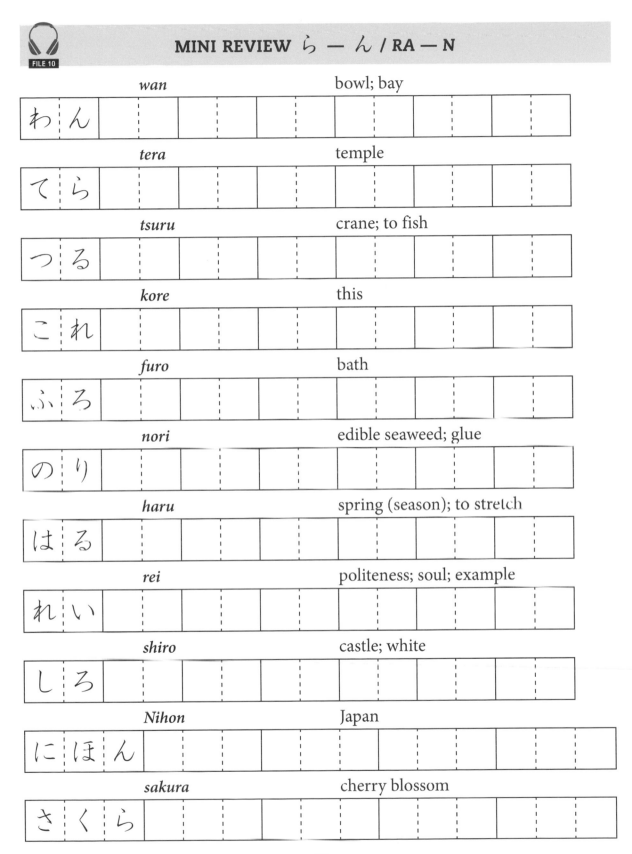

wan		bowl; bay
わ ん		

tera		temple
て ら		

tsuru		crane; to fish
つ る		

kore		this
こ れ		

furo		bath
ふ ろ		

nori		edible seaweed; glue
の り		

haru		spring (season); to stretch
は る		

rei		politeness; soul; example
れ い		

shiro		castle; white
し ろ		

Nihon		Japan
に ほ ん		

sakura		cherry blossom
さ く ら		

uchiwa　　　　　round fan

うちわ

matsuri　　　　festival

まつり

hotaru　　　　firefly

ほたる

futon　　　　futon

ふとん

rekishi　　　　history

れきし

wafuku　　　　Japanese clothing

わふく

riron　　　　theory

りろん

furoshiki　　　　cloth wrapper for parcels

ふろしき

harakiri　　　　hara-kiri

はらきり

hinomaru　　　　Rising Sun flag

ひのまる

samurai　　　　samurai

さむらい

VOICED AND HALF-VOICED SOUNDS

FILE 11

ga   as "ga" in "garden" but shorter

が												

gi   as "gee" in "geese" but shorter

ぎ												

gu   as "goo" in "goose" but shorter

ぐ												

ge   as "ge" in "get"

げ												

go   as "go" in "gore" but shorter

ご												

za   as "za" in "bizarre" but shorter

ざ												

ji   as "jee" in "jeep" but shorter

じ												

zu   as "zoo" but shorter

ず												

ze   as "ze" in "zest"

ぜ												

zo   as "zo" in "Azores" but shorter

ぞ												

da   as "da" in "dark" but shorter

だ												

ji   as "jee" in "jeep" but shorter

ぢ												

zu   as "zoo" but shorter

づ												

de   as "de" in "desk"

で												

do   as "doo" in "door" but shorter

ど												

ba   as "ba" in "bark" but shorter   *pa*   as "pa" in "park" but shorter

ば						ぱ						

bi   as "bea" in "beak" but shorter   *pi*   as "pea" in "peak" but shorter

び						ぴ						

bu   as "boo" in "boot" but shorter   *pu*   as "poo" in "pool" but shorter

ぶ						ぷ						

be   as "be" in "beg"   *pe*   as "pe" in "peg"

べ						ぺ						

bo   as "bo" in "bore" but shorter   *po*   as "po" in "pork" but shorter

ぼ						ぽ						

REVIEW OF VOICED AND HALF-VOICED SOUNDS

FILE 12

obi — waist sash for kimono

お び

fude — writing brush

ふ で

Zen — Zen

ぜ ん

soba — buckwheat noodles; side

そ ば

biwa — lute; loquat

び わ

geta — wooden clogs

げ た

Obon — Buddhist festival

お ぼ ん

Kabuki — Kabuki drama

か ぶ き

ojigi — bow (with the head)

お じ ぎ

sanpo — walk, stroll

さ ん ぽ

monpe — traditional work pants

も ん ぺ

keigo   polite language

けいご

mikado   old word for emperor

みかど

manga   comic strip

まんが

mikuji   written oracle

みくじ

yakuza   gangster

やくざ

nigiri   rice ball

にぎり

tengu   long-nosed goblin

てんぐ

hanaji   nosebleed

はなぢ

mizuwari   whisky and water

みずわり

zonjiru   know, believe

ぞんじる

daibutsu   large statue of Buddha

だいぶつ

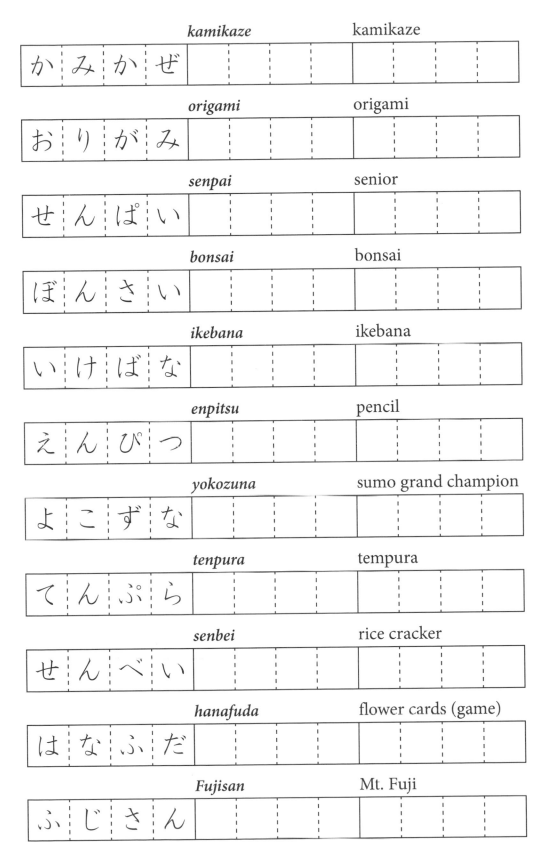

kamikaze — kamikaze

かみかぜ

origami — origami

おりがみ

senpai — senior

せんぱい

bonsai — bonsai

ぼんさい

ikebana — ikebana

いけばな

enpitsu — pencil

えんぴつ

yokozuna — sumo grand champion

よこずな

tenpura — tempura

てんぷら

senbei — rice cracker

せんべい

hanafuda — flower cards (game)

はなふだ

Fujisan — Mt. Fuji

ふじさん

REVIEW OF DOUBLE VOWELS AND CONSONANTS

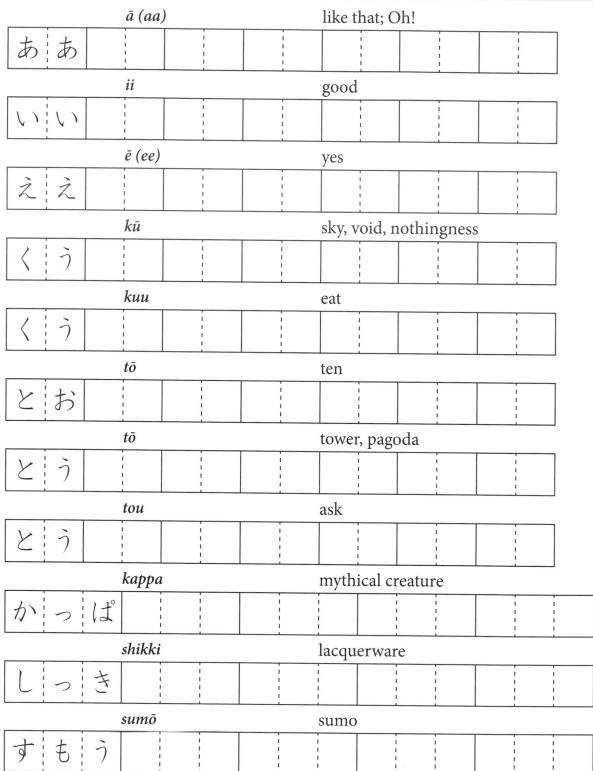

ā (aa)   like that; Oh!

あ　あ

ii   good

い　い

ē (ee)   yes

え　え

kū   sky, void, nothingness

く　う

kuu   eat

く　う

tō   ten

と　お

tō   tower, pagoda

と　う

tou   ask

と　う

kappa   mythical creature

か　っ　ぱ

shikki   lacquerware

し　っ　き

sumō   sumo

す　も　う

54

zōri — sandals

ぞ　う　り

sūji — numeral

す　う　じ

yūgen — tranquil beauty

ゆ　う　げ　ん

gakkō — school

が　っ　こ　う

kōyō — red leaves

こ　う　よ　う

ōkii — big

お　お　き　い

kendō — kendo

け　ん　ど　う

jingū — shrine

じ　ん　ぐ　う

fūrin — wind chime

ふ　う　り　ん

Shintō — Shinto

し　ん　と　う

kūkō — airport

く　う　こ　う

COMBINED SOUNDS KYA — RYO / きゃ ー りょ

FILE 14

kya

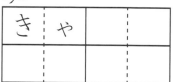

kyu

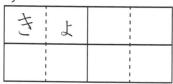

kyo

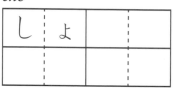

sha

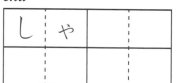

shu

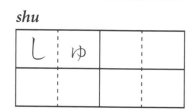

sho

cha

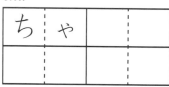

chu

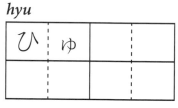

cho

nya

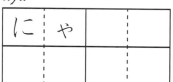

nyu

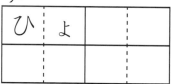

nyo

hya

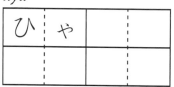

hyu

hyo

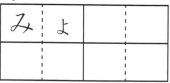

mya

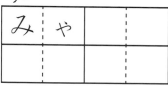

myu

myo

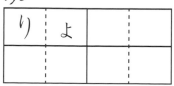

rya

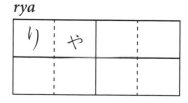

ryu

ryo

VOICED COMBINED SOUNDS GYA — BYO / ぎゃ — びょ

FILE 15

gya

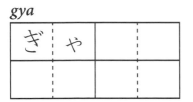

gyu

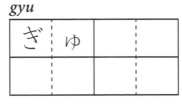

gyo

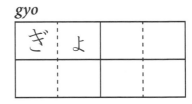

ja

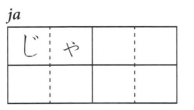

ju

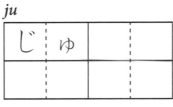

jo

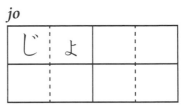

ja

ju

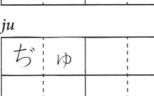

jo

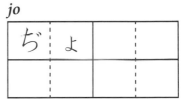

bya

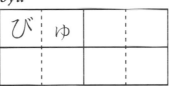

byu

byo

HALF-VOICED COMBINED SOUNDS PYA — PYO / ぴゃ — ぴょ

pya

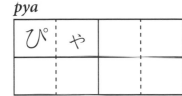

pyu

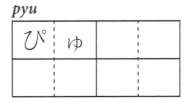

pyo

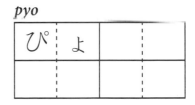

REVIEW OF COMBINED SOUNDS

kyaku   guest, visitor

き	ゃ	く						

shōji   sliding screen

し	ょ	う	じ			

byōbu   folding screen

び	ょ	う	ぶ			

jinja   shrine

じ	ん	じ	ゃ			

chanoyu   tea ceremony

ち	ゃ	の	ゆ		

geisha   geisha

げ	い	し	ゃ		

shodō   calligraphy

し	ょ	ど	う		

yakyū   baseball

や	き	ゅ	う		

enryo   reserve, restraint

え	ん	り	ょ		

myōji   family name

み	ょ	う	じ		

kingyo   goldfish

き	ん	ぎ	ょ		

REVIEW OF COMBINED SOUNDS

nyūshi entrance examination

に ゅ う し

Jukyō Confucianism

じ ゅ き ょ う

chōchin paper lantern

ち ょ う ち ん

hyōzan iceberg

ひ ょ う ざ ん

ryūgaku overseas study

り ゅ う が く

kōjō factory

こ う じ ょ う

jūdō judo

じ ゅ う ど う

Bukkyō Buddhism

ぶ っ き ょ う

shōgun shogun

し ょ う ぐ ん

nyōbō wife

に ょ う ぼ う

happyō announcement

は っ ぴ ょ う

REVIEW THROUGH JAPANESE HISTORICAL PERIODS

FILE 17

Jōmon   ca. 8000 BC – ca. 250 BC

じょうもん

Yayoi   ca. 250 BC – ca. AD 250

やよい

Nara   710–794

なら

Heian   794–1185

へいあん

Kamakura   1185–1333

かまくら

Muromachi   1392–1573

むろまち

Edo   1603–1868

えど

Meiji   1868–1912

めいじ

Taishō   1912–1926

だいしょう

Shōwa   1926–1989

しょうわ

Heisei   1989–

へいせい

GENERAL REVIEW

Nō   Noh drama

の	う								

sabi   elegant simplicity; rust

さ	び								

semi   cicada

せ	み								

giri   duty, honor

ぎ	り								

tako   kite; octopus

た	こ								

hakama   divided skirt

は	か	ま							

urushi   lacquer

う	る	し							

honne   one's real intent

ほ	ん	ね							

kokeshi   stylized wooden doll

こ	け	し							

haniwa   clay figurine

は	に	わ							

udon   wheat noodles

う	ど	ん							

kotatsu — brazier, foot warmer

こたつ

amae — childlike dependence

あまえ

Ebisu — name of god of wealth

えびす

miai — interview for marriage

みあい

tōfu — tofu

とうふ

seibo — year-end gift

せいぼ

shibumi — astringency

しぶみ

aware — pathos

あわれ

gohan — meal, cooked rice

ごはん

gagaku — ancient court music

ががく

noren — shop curtain

のれん

haori   short coat

| は | お | り | | | | | | | | | | |

meishi   name card

| め | い | し | | | | | | | | | | |

odori   dance

| お | ど | り | | | | | | | | | | |

kaisha   company

| か | い | し | ゃ | | | | | | |

menboku   reputation, "face"

| め | ん | ぼ | く | | | | | | |

shinju   pearl

| し | ん | じ | ゅ | | | | | | |

mugicha   barley tea

| む | ぎ | ち | ゃ | | | | | | |

tennō   emperor

| て | ん | の | う | | | | | | |

shōgi   Japanese chess

| し | ょ | う | ぎ | | | | | | |

onsen   hot spring

| お | ん | せ | ん | | | | | | |

misoshiru   miso soup

| み | そ | し | る | | | | | | |

ninja　　　ninja

に	ん	じ	ゃ								

tokonoma　　　decorative alcove

と	こ	の	ま								

soroban　　　abacus

そ	ろ	ば	ん								

bunraku　　　puppet theater

ぶ	ん	ら	く								

bentō　　　box lunch

べ	ん	と	う								

dantai　　　group

だ	ん	た	い								

shamisen　　　samisen

し	ゃ	み	せ	ん										

Shōgatsu　　　New Year

し	ょ	う	が	つ										

shakuhachi　　　flute

し	ゃ	く	は	ち										

koinobori　　　carp streamer

こ	い	の	ぼ	り										

janken　　　"scissors-paper-stone" game

じ	ゃ	ん	け	ん										

PART II
Katakana

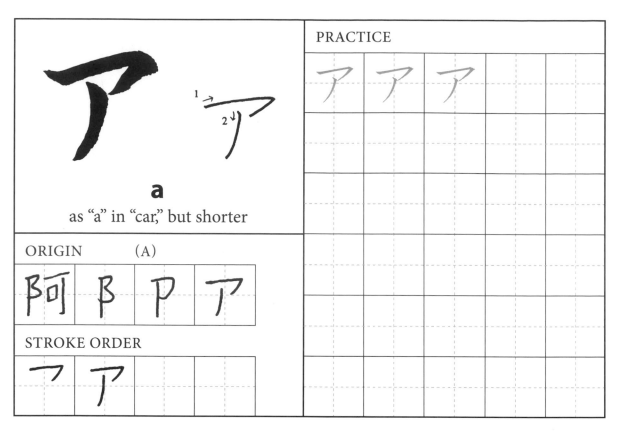

PRACTICE					

a

as "a" in "car," but shorter

ORIGIN (A)

STROKE ORDER

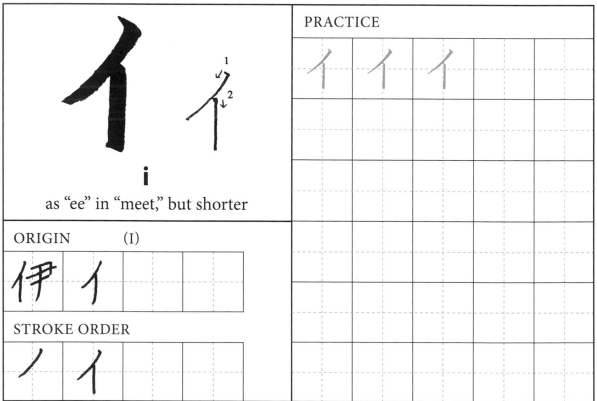

PRACTICE					

i

as "ee" in "meet," but shorter

ORIGIN (I)

STROKE ORDER

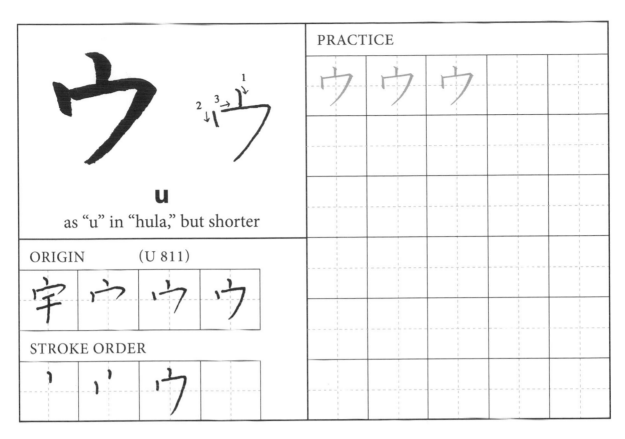

u

as "u" in "hula," but shorter

ORIGIN   (U 811)

STROKE ORDER

PRACTICE

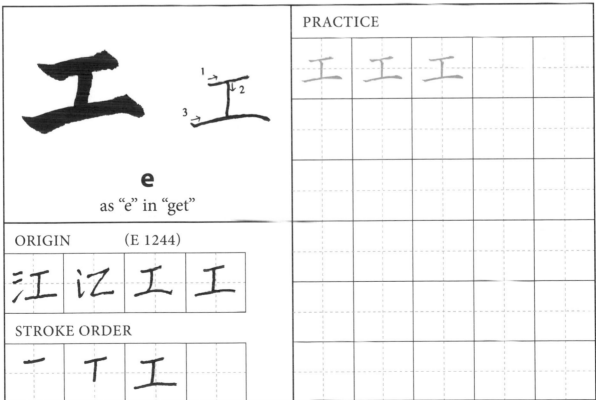

e

as "e" in "get"

ORIGIN   (E 1244)

STROKE ORDER

PRACTICE

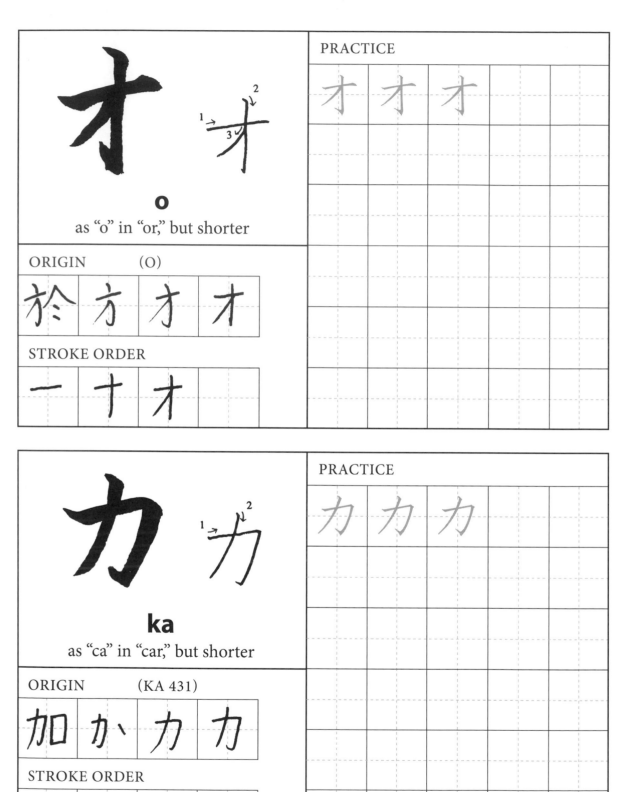

o

as "o" in "or," but shorter

ORIGIN   (O)

STROKE ORDER

PRACTICE

ka

as "ca" in "car," but shorter

ORIGIN   (KA 431)

STROKE ORDER

PRACTICE

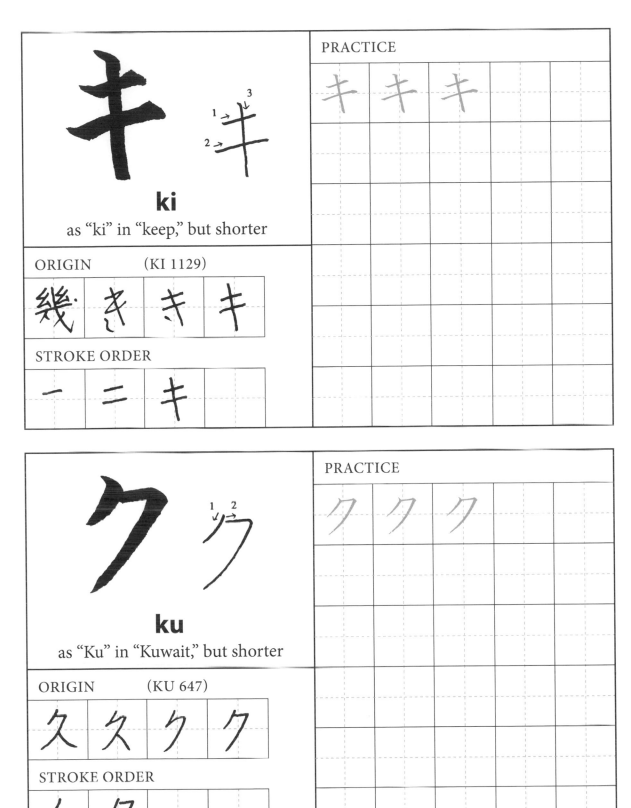

ki

as "ki" in "keep," but shorter

ORIGIN (KI 1129)

STROKE ORDER

PRACTICE

ku

as "Ku" in "Kuwait," but shorter

ORIGIN (KU 647)

STROKE ORDER

PRACTICE

ke

as "ke" in "keg"

ORIGIN   (KAI 1059)

STROKE ORDER

PRACTICE

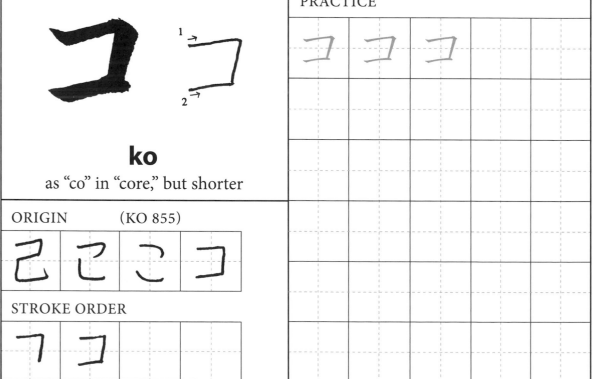

ko

as "co" in "core," but shorter

ORIGIN   (KO 855)

STROKE ORDER

PRACTICE

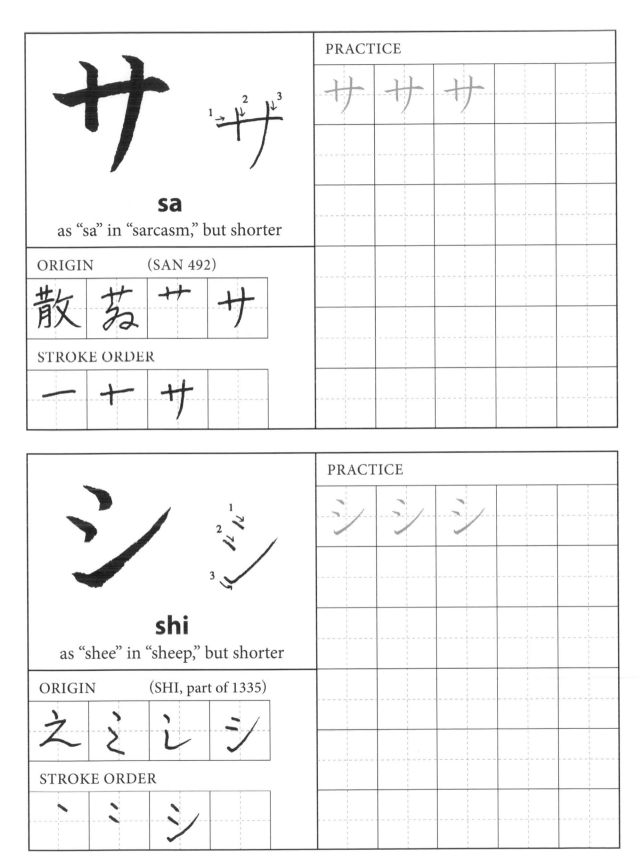

sa

as "sa" in "sarcasm," but shorter

ORIGIN   (SAN 492)

STROKE ORDER

PRACTICE

shi

as "shee" in "sheep," but shorter

ORIGIN   (SHI, part of 1335)

STROKE ORDER

PRACTICE

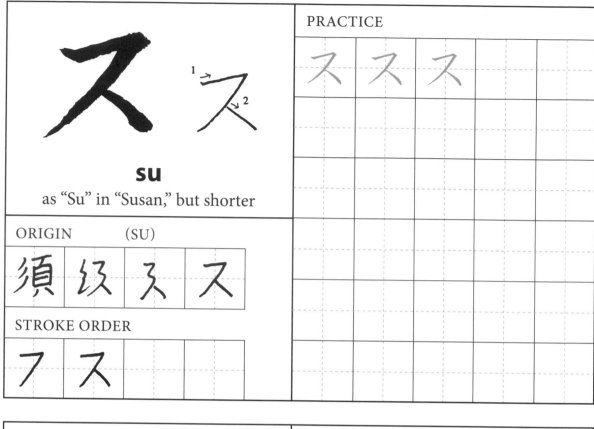

su

as "Su" in "Susan," but shorter

ORIGIN   (SU)

STROKE ORDER

PRACTICE

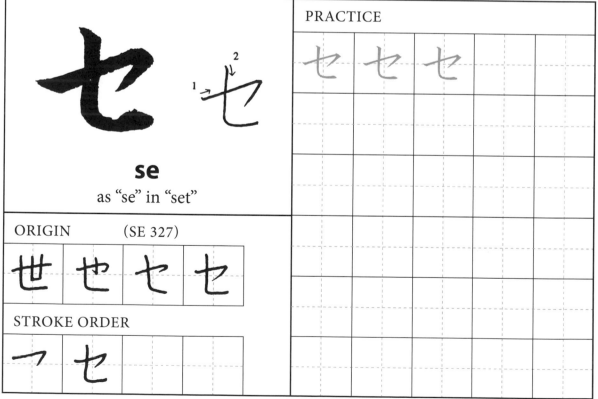

se

as "se" in "set"

ORIGIN   (SE 327)

STROKE ORDER

PRACTICE

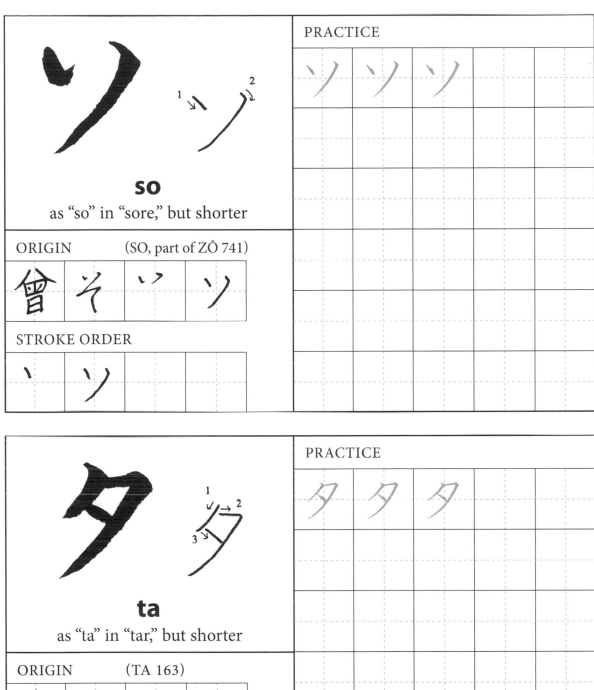

so

as "so" in "sore," but shorter

ORIGIN   (SO, part of ZŌ 741)

STROKE ORDER

PRACTICE

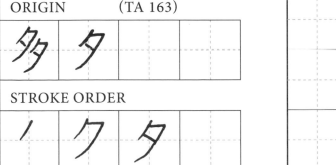

ta

as "ta" in "tar," but shorter

ORIGIN   (TA 163)

STROKE ORDER

PRACTICE

chi

as "chee" in "cheek," but shorter

ORIGIN   (CHI 47)

STROKE ORDER

PRACTICE

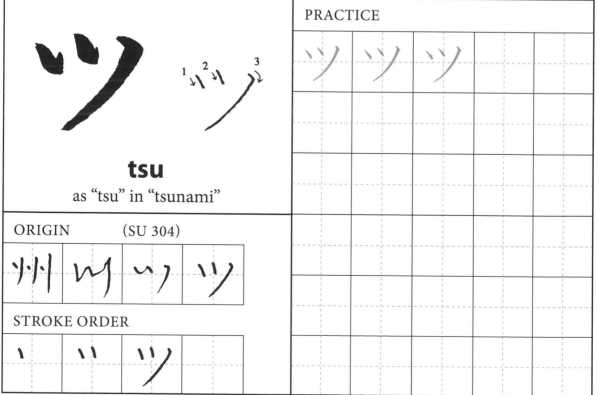

tsu

as "tsu" in "tsunami"

ORIGIN   (SU 304)

STROKE ORDER

PRACTICE

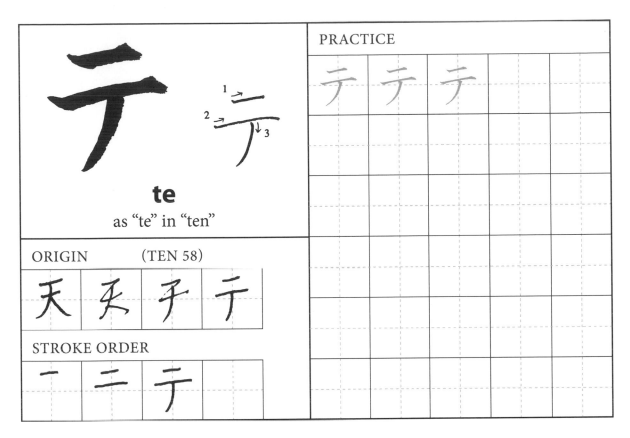

te

as "te" in "ten"

ORIGIN   (TEN 58)

STROKE ORDER

PRACTICE

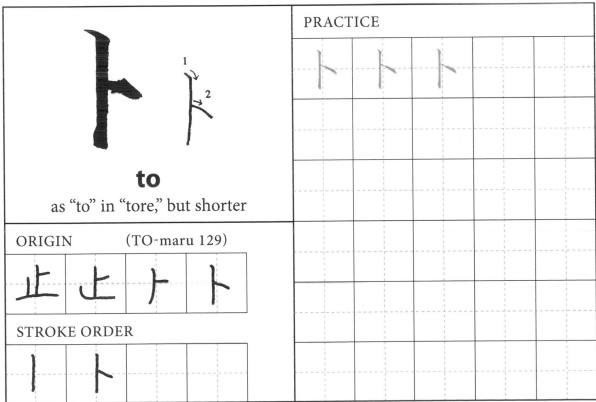

to

as "to" in "tore," but shorter

ORIGIN   (TO-maru 129)

STROKE ORDER

PRACTICE

MINI REVIEW アート / A—TO

FILE 19

katsu   cutlet

カ ツ

aisu   ice

ア イ ス

ēsu   ace

エ ー ス

kēki   cake

ケ ー キ

auto   out (baseball)

ア ウ ト

sāchi   search

サ ー チ

kōto   coat; court (sports)

コ ー ト

tsuā   tour

ツ ア ー

tesuto   test

テ ス ト

shītsu   sheet (bed)

シ ー ツ

sekuto   sect

セ ク ト

kōchi   coach (sports)

コ	ー	チ									

sōsu   sauce

ソ	ー	ス									

sukī   ski, skiing

ス	キ	ー									

takushī   taxi

タ	ク	シ	ー						

sutēki   steak

ス	テ	ー	キ						

sētā   sweater

セ	ー	タ	ー						

sākasu   circus

サ	ー	カ	ス						

ōkē   okay

オ	ー	ケ	ー						

ēkā   acre

エ	ー	カ	ー						

akashia   acacia

ア	カ	シ	ア						

sukēto   skate, skating

ス	ケ	ー	ト						

77

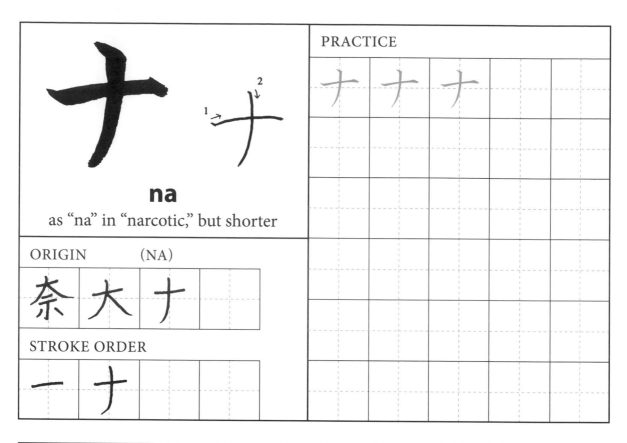

na

as "na" in "narcotic," but shorter

ORIGIN   (NA)

奈　大　ナ

STROKE ORDER

一　ナ

PRACTICE

ナ　ナ　ナ

ni

as "nea" in "neat," but shorter

ORIGIN   (NI 61)

二　二

STROKE ORDER

一　二

PRACTICE

二　二　二

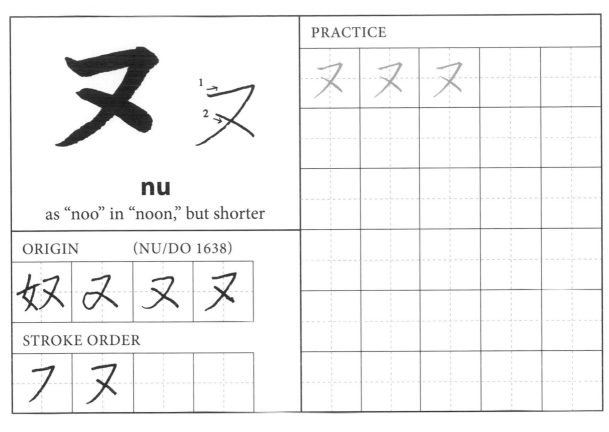

nu

as "noo" in "noon," but shorter

ORIGIN (NU/DO 1638)

STROKE ORDER

PRACTICE

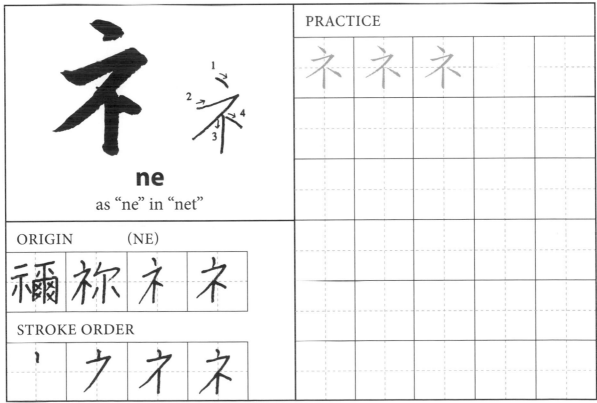

ne

as "ne" in "net"

ORIGIN (NE)

STROKE ORDER

PRACTICE

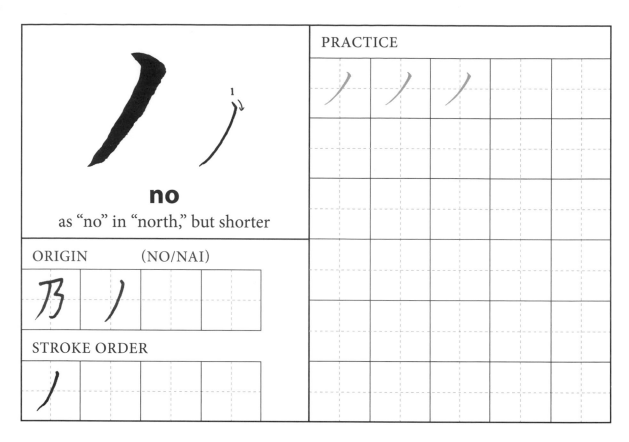

no

as "no" in "north," but shorter

ORIGIN   (NO/NAI)

STROKE ORDER

PRACTICE

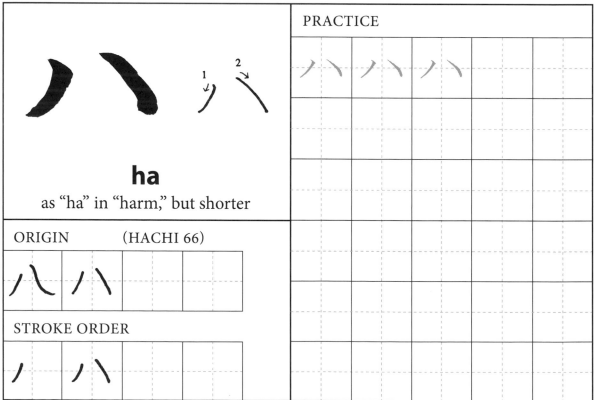

ha

as "ha" in "harm," but shorter

ORIGIN   (HACHI 66)

STROKE ORDER

PRACTICE

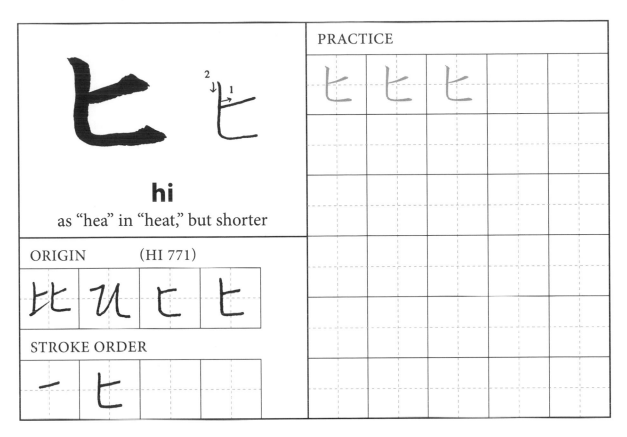

hi

as "hea" in "heat," but shorter

ORIGIN   (HI 771)

STROKE ORDER

PRACTICE

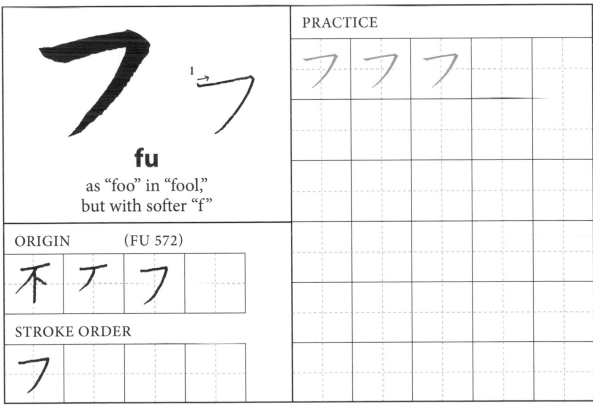

fu

as "foo" in "fool,"
but with softer "f"

ORIGIN   (FU 572)

STROKE ORDER

PRACTICE

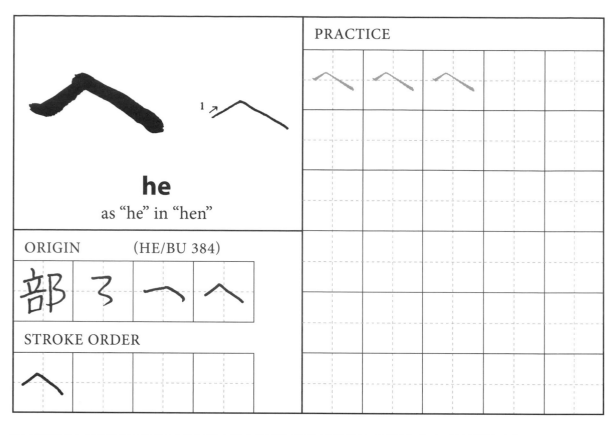

he

as "he" in "hen"

ORIGIN   (HE/BU 384)

STROKE ORDER

PRACTICE

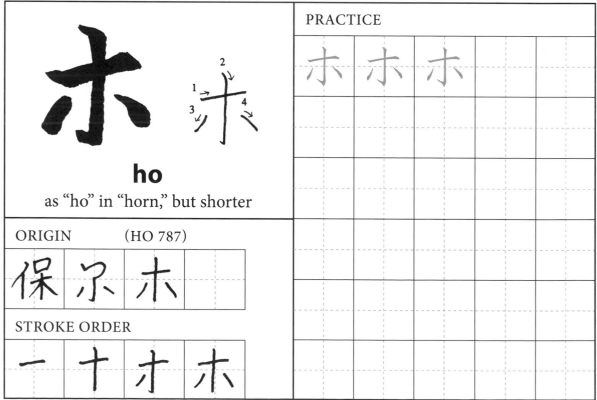

ho

as "ho" in "horn," but shorter

ORIGIN   (HO 787)

STROKE ORDER

PRACTICE

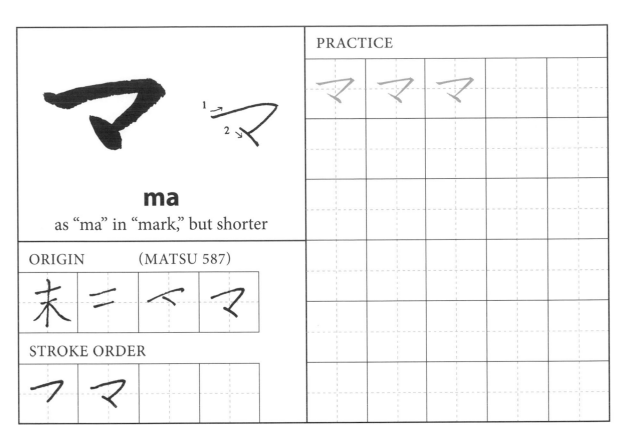

ma

as "ma" in "mark," but shorter

ORIGIN (MATSU 587)

STROKE ORDER

PRACTICE

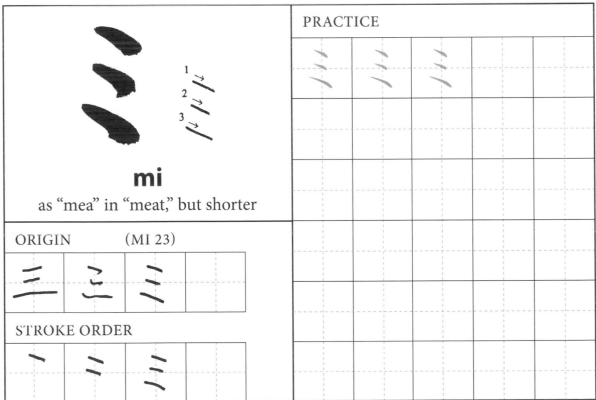

mi

as "mea" in "meat," but shorter

ORIGIN (MI 23)

STROKE ORDER

PRACTICE

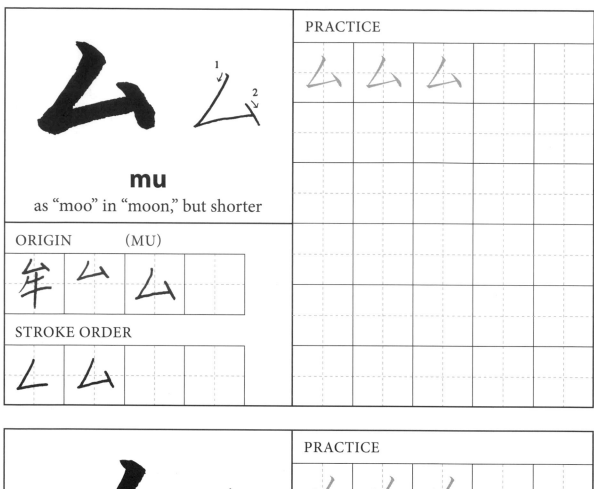

mu

as "moo" in "moon," but shorter

ORIGIN   (MU)

STROKE ORDER

PRACTICE

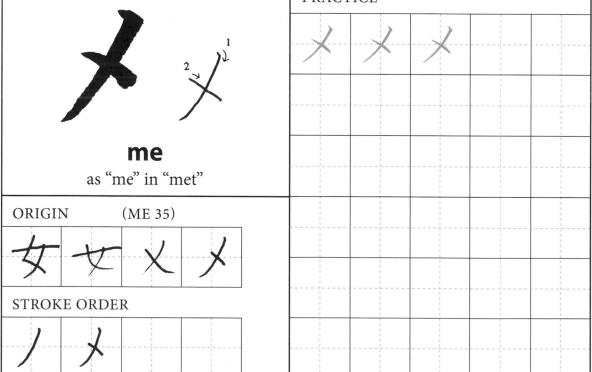

me

as "me" in "met"

ORIGIN   (ME 35)

STROKE ORDER

PRACTICE

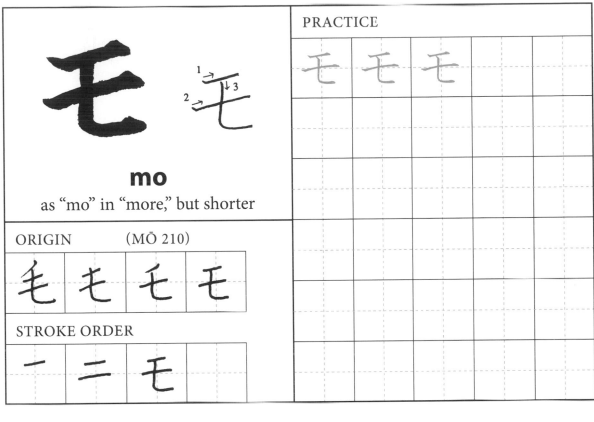

mo

as "mo" in "more," but shorter

ORIGIN   (MŌ 210)

STROKE ORDER

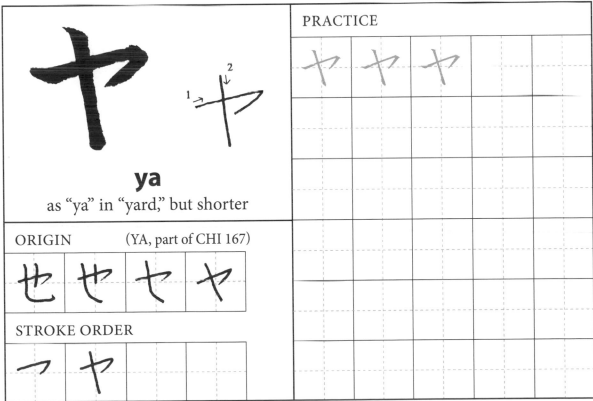

ya

as "ya" in "yard," but shorter

ORIGIN   (YA, part of CHI 167)

STROKE ORDER

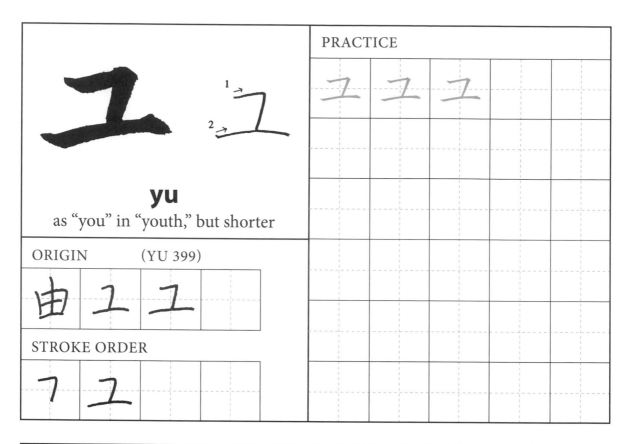

yu

as "you" in "youth," but shorter

ORIGIN   (YU 399)

STROKE ORDER

PRACTICE

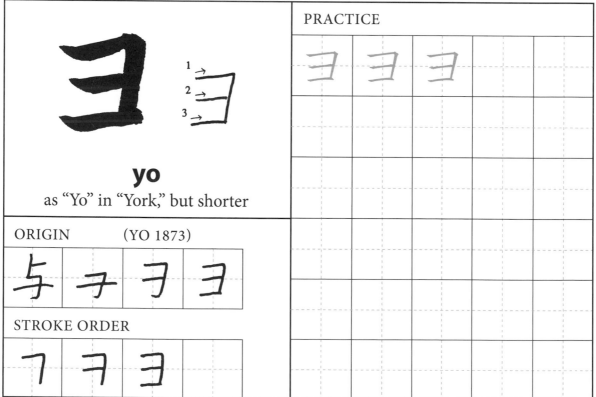

yo

as "Yo" in "York," but shorter

ORIGIN   (YO 1873)

STROKE ORDER

PRACTICE

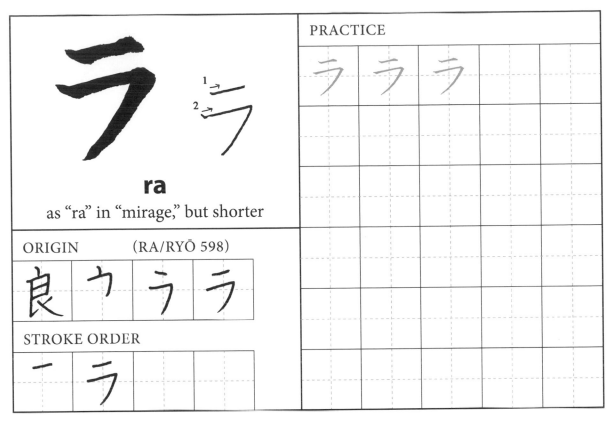

ra

as "ra" in "mirage," but shorter

ORIGIN   (RA/RYŌ 598)

STROKE ORDER

PRACTICE

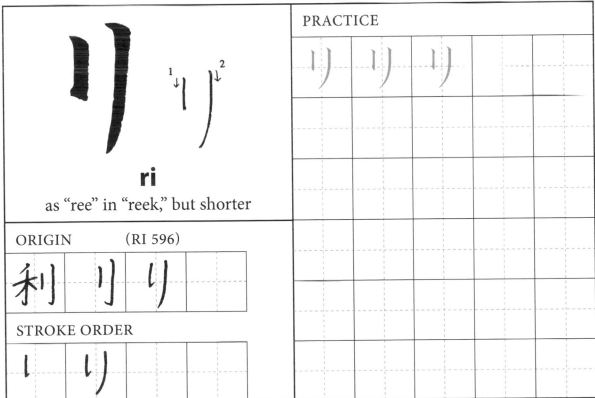

ri

as "ree" in "reek," but shorter

ORIGIN   (RI 596)

STROKE ORDER

PRACTICE

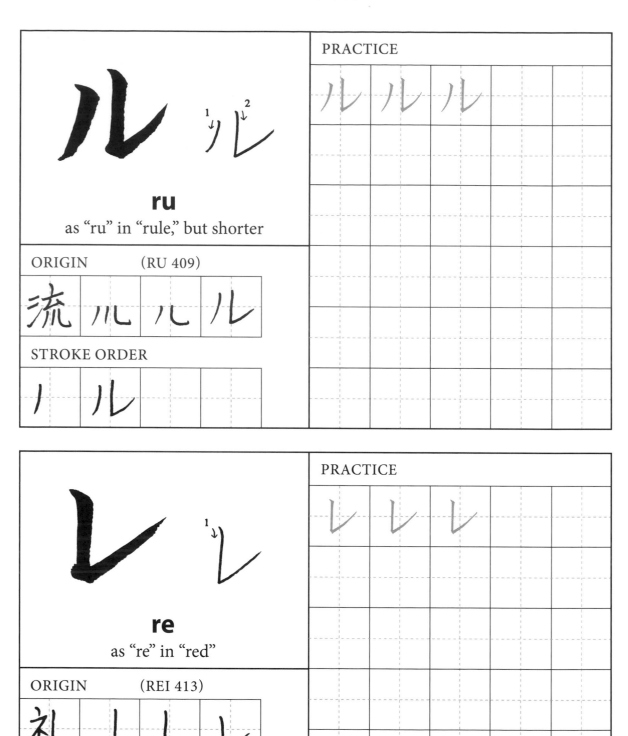

ル

ru

as "ru" in "rule," but shorter

PRACTICE

ルルル

ORIGIN   (RU 409)

流 ル ル ル

STROKE ORDER

ノ ル

レ

re

as "re" in "red"

PRACTICE

レ レ レ

ORIGIN   (REI 413)

礼 レ レ レ

STROKE ORDER

レ

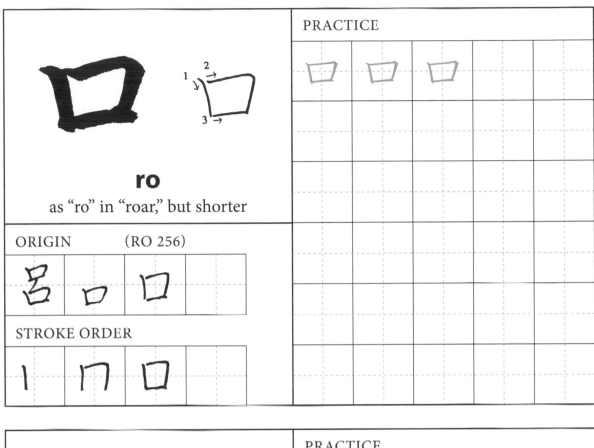

ro

as "ro" in "roar," but shorter

ORIGIN (RO 256)

STROKE ORDER

PRACTICE

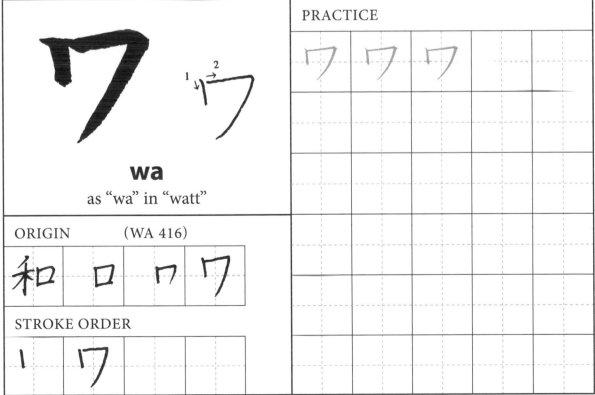

wa

as "wa" in "watt"

ORIGIN (WA 416)

STROKE ORDER

PRACTICE

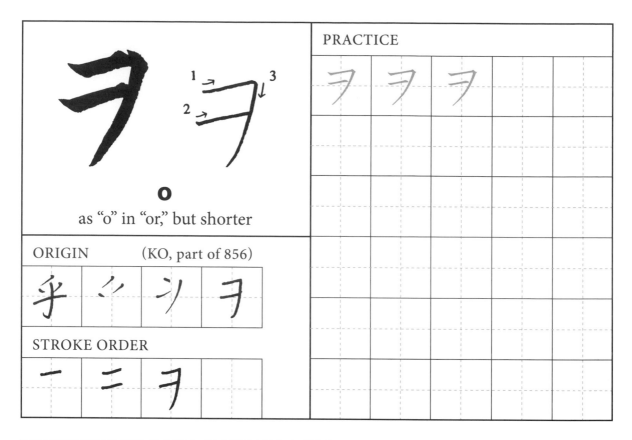

o

as "o" in "or," but shorter

ORIGIN   (KO, part of 856)

STROKE ORDER

PRACTICE

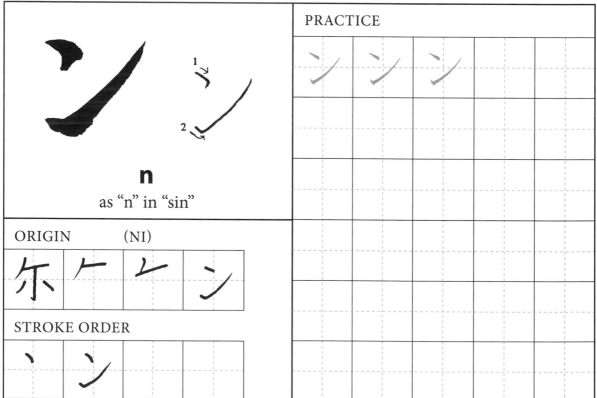

n

as "n" in "sin"

ORIGIN   (NI)

STROKE ORDER

PRACTICE

MINI REVIEW ナ ー ン / NA — N

FILE 20

heri — helicopter

ヘ | リ

memo — memo

メ | モ

hire — fillet

ヒ | レ

miruku — milk

ミ | ル | ク

kanū — canoe

カ | ヌ | ー

wanisu — varnish

ワ | ニ | ス

rōn — loan

ロ | ー | ン

naifu — knife

ナ | イ | フ

furē — Hooray!

フ | レ | ー

nōto — note, notebook

ノ | ー | ト

taiya — tire (car)

タ | イ | ヤ

kamera   camera

カ メ ラ

nēmu   name, reputation

ネ ー ム

yūmoa   humor

ユ ー モ ア

mainasu   minus

マ イ ナ ス

sararī   salary

サ ラ リ ー

hanmā   hammer

ハ ン マ ー

yōyō   yoyo

ヨ ー ヨ ー

hankachi   handkerchief

ハ ン カ チ

yunīku   unique

ユ ニ ー ク

nekutai   necktie

ネ ク タ イ

hōmuran   home run

ホ ー ム ラ ン

VOICED AND HALF-VOICED SOUNDS

ga   as "ga" in "garden" but shorter

ガ												

gi   as "gee" in "geese" but shorter

ギ												

gu   as "goo" in "goose" but shorter

グ												

ge   as "ge" in "get"

ゲ												

go   as "go" in "gore" but shorter

ゴ												

za   as "za" in "bizarre" but shorter

ザ												

ji   as "jee" in "jeep" but shorter

ジ												

zu   as "zoo" but shorter

ズ												

ze   as "ze" in "zest"

ゼ												

zo   as "zo" in "Azores" but shorter

ゾ												

da   as "da" in "dark" but shorter

ダ											

ji   as "jee" in "jeep" but shorter

チ											

zu   as "zoo" but shorter

ヅ											

de   as "de" in "desk"

デ											

do   as "doo" in "door" but shorter

ド											

ba   as "ba" in "bark" but shorter   *pa*   as "pa" in "park" but shorter

バ					パ					

bi   as "bea" in "beak" but shorter   *pi*   as "pea" in "peak" but shorter

ビ					ピ					

bu   as "boo" in "boot" but shorter   *pu*   as "poo" in "pool" but shorter

ブ					プ					

be   as "be" in "beg"   *pe*   as "pe" in "peg"

ベ					ペ					

bo   as "bo" in "bore" but shorter   *po*   as "po" in "pork" but shorter

ボ					ポ					

REVIEW OF VOICED AND HALF-VOICED SOUNDS

FILE 21

biru   building

ビ ル

zero   zero

ゼ ロ

basu   bus; bath

バ ス

giya   gear

ギ ヤ

dansu   dance

ダ ン ス

gēmu   game

ゲ ー ム

gaido   guide; guidebook

ガ イ ド

gorufu   golf

ゴ ル フ

bēsu   base

ベ ー ス

zubon   trousers

ズ ボ ン

gorira   gorilla

ゴ リ ラ

daburu　double

ダ　ブ　ル

zōn　zone

ゾ　ー　ン

jiguzagu　zigzag

ジ　グ　ザ　グ

repōto　report

レ　ポ　ー　ト

jīnzu　jeans

ジ　ー　ン　ズ

wāpuro　word processor

ワ　ー　プ　ロ

pachinko　Japanese pinball

パ　チ　ン　コ

dezāto　dessert

デ　ザ　ー　ト

pīman　green pepper

ピ　ー　マ　ン

mai pēsu　at one's own speed ("my pace")

マ　イ　ペ　ー　ス

arubaito　part-time job

ア　ル　バ　イ　ト

COMBINED SOUNDS KYA — RYO / キャ ― リョ

kya

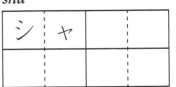

kyu

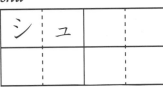

kyo

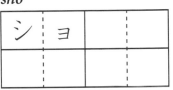

sha

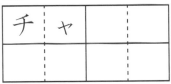

shu

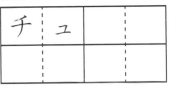

sho

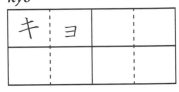

cha

chu

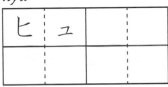

cho

nya

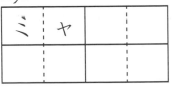

nyu

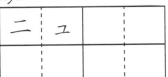

nyo

hya

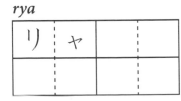

hyu

hyo

mya

myu

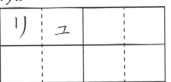

myo

rya

ryu

ryo

VOICED COMBINED SOUNDS GYA — BYO / ギャ — ビョ

gya

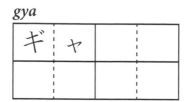

gyu

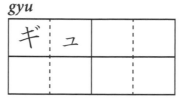

gyo

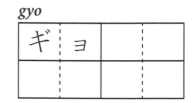

ja

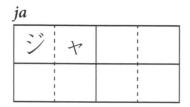

ju

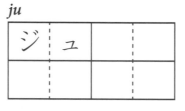

jo

ja

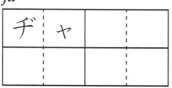

ju

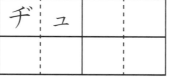

jo

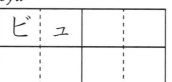

bya

byu

byo

HALF-VOICED COMBINED SOUNDS PYA — PYO / ピャ — ピョ

pya

pyu

pyo

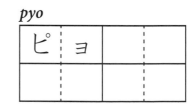

REVIEW OF COMBINED SOUNDS AND DOUBLE CONSONANTS

FILE 22

shō　　　　　show

シ ョ ー

netto　　　　net

ネ ッ ト

fan　　　　　fan (sports)

フ ァ ン

yeti　　　　　yeti

イ エ テ ィ

nyūsu　　　　news

ニ ュ ー ス

fōku　　　　fork; folk

フ ォ ー ク

chekku　　　　check

チ ェ ッ ク

jerī　　　　jelly

ジ ェ リ ー

chōku　　　　chalk

チ ョ ー ク

wotchi　　　　watch

ウ ォ ッ チ

disuku　　　　disk

デ ィ ス ク

fairu   file

ファ イ ル

wēbu/wēvu   wave (hair)

ウ ェ ー ヴ

bideo/video   video

ヴ ィ デ オ

manshon   apartment house

マ ン シ ョ ン

windō   window

ウ ィ ン ド ー

mājan   mah-jong

マ ー ジ ャ ン

wētā   waiter

ウ エ ー タ ー

kyasshu   cash

キ ャ ッ シ ュ

hyūman   human

ヒ ュ ー マ ン

pitchā   pitcher (sports)

ピ ッ チ ャ ー

duetto   duet

ヂ ュ エ ッ ト

FILE 23

REVIEW THROUGH CONTINENT AND COUNTRY NAMES

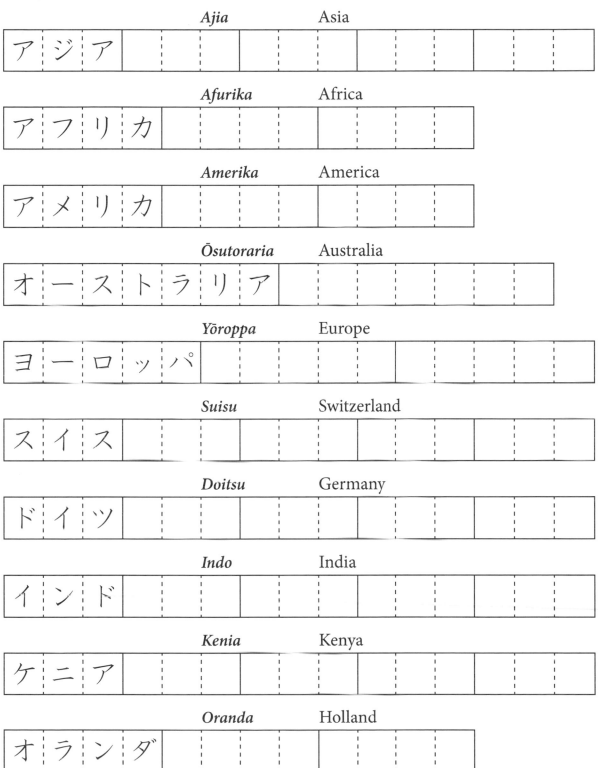

Ajia   Asia

アジア

Afurika   Africa

アフリカ

Amerika   America

アメリカ

Ōsutoraria   Australia

オーストラリア

Yōroppa   Europe

ヨーロッパ

Suisu   Switzerland

スイス

Doitsu   Germany

ドイツ

Indo   India

インド

Kenia   Kenya

ケニア

Oranda   Holland

オランダ

Igirisu   England

| イ | ギ | リ | ス |

Mekishiko   Mexico

| メ | キ | シ | コ |

Betonamu   Vietnam

| ベ | ト | ナ | ム |

Kyūba   Cuba

| キ | ュ | ー | バ |

Furansu   France

| フ | ラ | ン | ス |

Ejiputo   Egypt

| エ | ジ | プ | ト |

Firipin   Philippines

| フ | ィ | リ | ピ | ン |

Echiopia   Ethiopa

| エ | チ | オ | ピ | ア |

Noruwē   Norway

| ノ | ル | ウ | ェ | ー |

Chunijia   Tunisia

| チ | ュ | ニ | ジ | ア |

Marēshia   Malaysia

| マ | レ | ー | シ | ア |

PART III

Final Review

DO-IT-YOURSELF KANA CHARTS

Fill in the following charts, writing *hiragana* in the left part of each box and *katakana* in the right. Then check your entries against the charts in the "Explanation of *Kana*" on pages 9–11.

Basic Kana Symbols

VOWELS

	a	*i*	*u*	*e*	*o*
	a	*i*	*u*	*e*	*o*
k	*ka*	*ki*	*ku*	*ke*	*ko*
s	*sa*	*shi*	*su*	*se*	*so*
t	*ta*	*chi*	*tsu*	*te*	*to*
n	*na*	*ni*	*nu*	*ne*	*no*
h	*ha*	*hi*	*fu*	*he*	*ho*
m	*ma*	*mi*	*mu*	*me*	*mo*
y	*ya*		*yu*		*yo*
r	*ra*	*ri*	*ru*	*re*	*ro*
w	*wa*				*o*
n	*n*				

CONSONANTS

Basic Voiced Sounds

	a	i	u	e	o
g	ga	gi	gu	ge	go
z/j	za	ji	zu	ze	zo
d/z/j	da	ji	zu	de	do
b	ba	bi	bu	be	bo
p	pa	pi	pu	pe	po

Basic Combinations

	a	u	o
ky	kya	kyu	kyo
sh	sha	shu	sho
ch	cha	chu	cho
ny	nya	nyu	nyo
hy	hya	hyu	hyo
my	mya	myu	myo
ry	rya	ryu	ryo

Voiced Combinations

	a	u	o
gy	gya	gyu	gyo
j	ja	ju	jo
j	ja	ju	jo
by	bya	byu	byo
py	pya	pyu	pyo

FILE 24

JAPANESE PLACE NAMES QUIZ

Fill the blanks with the correct *kana* from the list on the facing page.

Cities

1. Tokyo _____
2. Sapporo _____
3. Sendai _____
4. Yokohama _____
5. Nagoya _____
6. Osaka _____
7. Hiroshima _____
8. Kyoto _____
9. Nagasaki _____
10. Kobe _____
11. Fukuoka _____

Islands and prefectures

1. Honshu _____
2. Chiba Prefecture _____
3. Kyushu _____
4. Hokkaido _____
5. Gifu Prefecture _____
6. Shikoku _____
7. Saitama Prefecture _____
8. Hyogo Prefecture _____
9. Kumamoto Prefecture _____
10. Kanagawa Prefecture _____
11. Okinawa _____

Tourist attractions

1. Nikko _____
2. Nijo Castle _____
3. Lake Biwa _____
4. Kiyomizu Temple _____
5. Kyoto Imperial Palace _____
6. Tokyo Imperial Palace _____
7. Mount Fuji _____
8. Tokyo Skytree _____
9. Meiji Shrine _____
10. Osaka Castle _____
11. Sensoji Temple _____

めいじじんぐう	よこはま	ふくおか
ふじさん	さいたまけん	せんだい
ぎふけん	ひろしま	おおさかじょう
ながさき	ひょうごけん	ほんしゅう
なごや	とうきょう	こうべ
にっこう	びわこ	きゅうしゅう
ちばけん	にじょうじょう	きょうと
せんそうじ	おきなわ	しこく
きよみずでら	かながわけん	ほっかいどう
こうきょ	さっぽろ	きょうとごしょ
くまもとけん	とうきょうスカイツリー	おおさか

FILE 25

INTERNATIONAL CITIES QUIZ

Use the first blank to copy the *katakana* city name and the second blank to give the name of the city in English. Be warned that Japanese renditions are usually based closely on the language of the country of the city in question.

1. ローマ　　　　　　　＿＿＿＿＿＿＿＿　＿＿＿＿＿＿＿＿
2. アテネ　　　　　　　＿＿＿＿＿＿＿＿　＿＿＿＿＿＿＿＿
3. プラハ　　　　　　　＿＿＿＿＿＿＿＿　＿＿＿＿＿＿＿＿
4. モスクワ　　　　　　＿＿＿＿＿＿＿＿　＿＿＿＿＿＿＿＿
5. シドニー　　　　　　＿＿＿＿＿＿＿＿　＿＿＿＿＿＿＿＿
6. ウィーン　　　　　　＿＿＿＿＿＿＿＿　＿＿＿＿＿＿＿＿
7. バグダッド　　　　　＿＿＿＿＿＿＿＿　＿＿＿＿＿＿＿＿
8. ジャカルタ　　　　　＿＿＿＿＿＿＿＿　＿＿＿＿＿＿＿＿
9. サンチアゴ　　　　　＿＿＿＿＿＿＿＿　＿＿＿＿＿＿＿＿
10. ハリウッド　　　　　＿＿＿＿＿＿＿＿　＿＿＿＿＿＿＿＿
11. ミュンヘン　　　　　＿＿＿＿＿＿＿＿　＿＿＿＿＿＿＿＿
12. ヴェネチア　　　　　＿＿＿＿＿＿＿＿　＿＿＿＿＿＿＿＿
13. ロンドン　　　　　　＿＿＿＿＿＿＿＿　＿＿＿＿＿＿＿＿
14. マニラ　　　　　　　＿＿＿＿＿＿＿＿　＿＿＿＿＿＿＿＿
15. ワシントン　　　　　＿＿＿＿＿＿＿＿　＿＿＿＿＿＿＿＿
16. ブエノスアイレス　　＿＿＿＿＿＿＿＿　＿＿＿＿＿＿＿＿
17. オークランド　　　　＿＿＿＿＿＿＿＿　＿＿＿＿＿＿＿＿
18. ナイロビ　　　　　　＿＿＿＿＿＿＿＿　＿＿＿＿＿＿＿＿
19. マドリード　　　　　＿＿＿＿＿＿＿＿　＿＿＿＿＿＿＿＿
20. クアラルンプール　　＿＿＿＿＿＿＿＿　＿＿＿＿＿＿＿＿
21. ニューヨーク　　　　＿＿＿＿＿＿＿＿　＿＿＿＿＿＿＿＿
22. リオデジャネイロ　　＿＿＿＿＿＿＿＿　＿＿＿＿＿＿＿＿
23. メルボルン　　　　　＿＿＿＿＿＿＿＿　＿＿＿＿＿＿＿＿

24. ヨハネスブルグ   _____   _____

25. カイロ   _____   _____

26. パース   _____   _____

27. リマ   _____   _____

28. サンフランシスコ   _____   _____

29. ニューデリー   _____   _____

30. ムンバイ   _____   _____

31. アムステルダム   _____   _____

32. カブール   _____   _____

33. マイアミ   _____   _____

34. サンパウロ   _____   _____

35. ホノルル   _____   _____

36. テルアビブ   _____   _____

37. イスタンブール   _____   _____

38. ケープタウン   _____   _____

39. モントリオール   _____   _____

40. パリ   _____   _____

41. ベルリン   _____   _____

42. バンコク   _____   _____

43. シンガポール   _____   _____

44. リスボン   _____   _____

45. オスロ   _____   _____

46. レィキャビク   _____   _____

47. アジスアベバ   _____   _____

48. マンチェスター   _____   _____

49. トロント   _____   _____

50. シカゴ   _____   _____

FILE 26

FLORA AND FAUNA QUIZ

Fill in the blanks with *hiragana* (H) or *katakana* (K) as appropriate.

1. *inu* (H)   ——————————————   dog

2. *sakana* (H)   ——————————————   fish

3. *raion* (K)   ——————————————   lion

4. *take* (H)   ——————————————   bamboo

5. *kaede* (H)   ——————————————   maple

6. *yūkari* (K)   ——————————————   eucalyptus

7. *tsubaki* (H)   ——————————————   camellia

8. *chūrippu* (K)   ——————————————   tulip

9. *maguro* (H)   ——————————————   tuna

10. *koara* (K)   ——————————————   koala bear

11. *nihonzaru* (H)   ——————————————   Japanese monkey

12. *kangarū* (K)   ——————————————   kangaroo

13. *nezumi* (H)   ——————————————   mouse, rat

14. *ajisai* (H)   ——————————————   hydrangea

15. *haibisukasu* (K)   ——————————————   hibiscus

16. *hyō* (H)   ——————————————   leopard

17. *kānēshon* (K)   ——————————————   carnation

18. *kabutomushi* (H)   ——————————————   Goliath beetle

19. *hebi* (H)   ——————————————   snake

20. *pengin* (K)   ——————————————   penguin

21. *hirame* (H)   ——————————————   flatfish

22. *botan* (H)   ——————————————   peony

23. *mahogani* (K)   ——————————————   mahogany

24. *suisen* (H)   ——————————————   narcissus

25. *ichō* (H)   ——————————————   gingko

PERSONAL NAMES QUIZ

Underline the *kana* error in each name and write the correct version in the blank.

1.	じろお	_____	Jiro (*Jirō*)
2.	キャロル	_____	Carole (*Kyaroru*)
3.	ねいこ	_____	Reiko
4.	ノームン	_____	Norman (*Nōman*)
5.	とるお	_____	Teruo
6.	ウェソディー	_____	Wendy (*Wendī*)
7.	まさよし	_____	Masayoshi
8.	ヴァヌサ	_____	Vanessa (*Vanesa*)
9.	おけみ	_____	Akemi
10.	ドワート	_____	Dwight (*Dowaito*)
11.	けんいし	_____	Kenichi (*Ken'ichi*)
12.	シェーノ	_____	Shane (*Shēn*)
13.	ゆきい	_____	Yukiko
14.	ヂエリー	_____	Julie (*Jurī*)
15.	おりへ	_____	Orie
16.	ソフェ	_____	Sophie (*Sofi*)
17.	っとむ	_____	Tsutomu
18.	ウイリマム	_____	William (*Wiriamu*)
19.	ひでミ	_____	Hidemi
20.	ジャッタ	_____	Jack (*Jakku*)
21.	されこ	_____	Sawako
22.	デヴィっド	_____	David (*Deibiddo*)
23.	のそむ	_____	Nozomu
24.	ェリザペス	_____	Elizabeth (*Erizabesu*)
25.	ラッセル	_____	Russell (*Rasseru*)

FOOD ITEMS QUIZ

Fill in the blanks with appropriate romanization

1.	てんぷら	_____	tempura
2.	おにぎり	_____	rice ball
3.	ラーメン	_____	ramen noodles
4.	カレーライス	_____	curry rice
5.	やきそば	_____	fried noodles
6.	とんかつ	_____	deep-fried pork cutlet
7.	ぎょうざ	_____	pan-fried dumpling
8.	えだまめ	_____	edamame beans
9.	うめぼし	_____	pickled plum
10.	みそしる	_____	miso soup
11.	たこやき	_____	octopus dumpling
12.	とうふ	_____	tofu
13.	オムレツ	_____	omelet
14.	しょうゆ	_____	soy sauce
15.	おべんとう	_____	box lunch
16.	ぶたにく	_____	pork
17.	ぎゅうにく	_____	beef
18.	とりにく	_____	chicken
19.	ヴェニソン	_____	venison
20.	さかな	_____	fish
21.	まぐろ	_____	tuna
22.	たまご	_____	egg
23.	やさい	_____	vegetable
24.	くだもの	_____	fruit

25.	りんご	_____	apple
26.	みかん	_____	mandarin orange
27.	パン	_____	bread
28.	チーズ	_____	cheese
29.	バター	_____	butter
30.	ハンバーグ	_____	hamburger
31.	スパゲティ	_____	spaghetti
32.	シチュー	_____	stew
33.	フライドポテト	_____	french fries
34.	サラダ	_____	salad
35.	かし	_____	confectionery
36.	ヨーグルト	_____	yogurt
37.	さとう	_____	sugar
38.	ビスケット	_____	biscuit
39.	パフェ	_____	parfait
40.	アイスクリーム	_____	ice cream
41.	プリン	_____	custard pudding
42.	チョコレート	_____	chocolate
43.	ビール	_____	beer
44.	ワイン	_____	wine
45.	にほんしゅ	_____	Japanese saké
46.	ジュース	_____	juice
47.	コーヒー	_____	coffee
48.	レモンティー	_____	lemon tea
49.	こうちゃ	_____	black tea
50.	おちゃ	_____	green tea

WORK AND PLAY QUIZ

Copy each word from the list at the bottom of the page under the correct heading, *Occupation* or *Pastime*, and write the English translation of each word next to it, using a dictionary if you need to.

Occupation

Kana   *English*

_____   _____

_____   _____

_____   _____

_____   _____

_____   _____

_____   _____

_____   _____

_____   _____

_____   _____

Pastime

Kana   *English*

_____   _____

_____   _____

_____   _____

_____   _____

_____   _____

_____   _____

_____   _____

_____   _____

_____   _____

やきゅう　　せんせい　　かんごし　　がくせい　　どくしょ　　ゴルフ

サーフィン　　いしゃ　　はいしゃ　　テレビゲーム　　ウェブデザイナー

べんごし　　いけばな　　バレーボール　　エンジニア　　カラオケ

じゅうどう　　おりがみ　　けんちくか　　ウエーター

FAMILY MEMBERS QUIZ

Draw a line to match each word to its *hiragana*, using a dictionary if necessary, then copy the *hiragana*.

1.	My* mother	ちち	_____
2.	Your** mother	あね	_____
3.	My father	きょうだい	_____
4.	Your father	はは	_____
5.	My older sister	おじいさん	_____
6.	Your older sister	おかあさん	_____
7.	Your younger sister	おとうさん	_____
8.	My younger sister	ごしゅじん	_____
9.	My older brother	おにいさん	_____
10.	Your older brother	いもうと	_____
11.	My younger brother	おとうとさん	_____
12.	Your younger brother	いもうとさん	_____
13.	Siblings	つま	_____
14.	My grandfather	おねえさん	_____
15.	Your grandfather	かぞく	_____
16.	My grandmother	おくさん	_____
17.	Your grandmother	おばあさん	_____
18.	My wife	そふ	_____
19.	Your wife	おとうと	_____
20.	My husband	あに	_____
21.	Your husband	そぼ	_____
22.	Family	おっと	_____

* The use of "my" here indicates the humble form of the word used when talking to others about one's own family members.

** The use of "your" here indicates the honorific form of the word used when talking to others about their family members. In some cases, this honorific is also used as a form of address.

ABOUT JAPAN

Copy each line in the space provided.

せかいちずをみましょう。にほんはア

ジアたいりくのひがしにある、なんぼくに

ほそながいくにです。そのひろさはアメリ

カのカリフォルニアしゅうとだいたいおな

じです。よっつのおもなしまにわかれてい

ます。いちばんおおきいのは、ほんしゅう

で、このしまのまんなかへんにとうきょう

があります。ふじさんという、うつくしい

やまもあります。にばんめにおおきしま

は、いちばんきたにあるほっかいどうで、

なつはすずしいですが、ふゆはさむくて、

ゆきがたくさんふりますから、スキーやス

ケートができます。さんばんめにおおきい

きゅうしゅうは、みなみにありますから、

ふゆでもあたたかいです。よんばんめのし

こくは、きたのほうはみかんで、みなみの

ほうはさかなで、ゆうめいです。

SELF-INTRODUCTION

Copy each line in the space provided. Then, using the photocopiable practice pages at the back of the book, use this self-introduction as a model to write about yourself.

わたしはソフィ・スミスです。オース

トラリアのシドニーにすんでいます。だい

がくでにほんごをべんきょうしています。

かぞくといっしょにシドニーのゆうめいな

ボンダイビーチにすんでいます。わたしは

ごにんかぞくです。ちちはいしゃです。

ははかんごしです。あにのデイビッドは

シーフード・レストランでウエーターとし

てはたらいています。いもうとのジェーン

はこうこうせいです。わたしのしゅみはサ

ーフィンです。だいがくをそつぎょうした

らにほんごのきょうしになりたいとおもっ

ています。

A TRIP ABROAD

Copy each line in the space provided. Then, using the photocopiable practice pages at the back of the book, use this piece of writing as a model to write about a trip you took.

きょねんはじめてにほんにいきまし

た。とてもたのしかったです。とうきょう

にはみっかかんいました。はらじゅくでか

いものをして、めいじじんぐうででんとう

てきなにほんのけっこんしきをみて、にほ

んのいちばんたかいビルのとうきょうスカ

イツリーにのぼりました。てんきがはれて

いたのでスカイツリーからふじさんがみえ

ました。とうきょうからしんかんせんできょ

うとまでいきました。きょうとのふるいお

てらはうつくしいです。いちばんすきなお

てらはきよみずでらでした。きょうとのりょ

うりはおいしくて、すしをたくさんたべま

した。

KANA WORD SEARCH

ヌ	カ	い	ル	イ	サ	ミ	ま	エ	ラ	ヤ	う	く	れ	プ
ご	う	ウ	り	め	ね	キ	な	ジ	こ	つ	ぞ	め	ロ	ぬ
モ	ぜ	な	ン	あ	ま	ウ	オ	け	と	わ	り	ぺ	ぼ	ぶ
よ	ね	ほ	る	ト	わ	ホ	に	ス	ぎ	さ	ラ	ど	す	し
ら	そ	し	ぷ	ネ	し	せ	ス	ど	ク	と	る	む	う	パ
い	わ	つ	め	ズ	う	ち	ま	テ	レ	ビ	か	ふ	べ	ぐ
ア	お	れ	ユ	で	ま	も	ざ	た	ル	ア	ん	シ	さ	か
よ	ろ	い	に	し	ワ	る	ネ	あ	に	ゾ	じ	い	ね	す
や	る	ば	ん	が	ル	ト	だ	ナ	が	ん	げ	も	ゴ	ケ
ず	み	き	メ	グ	ツ	ン	イ	て	し	ら	ち	デ	ニ	ム
の	プ	せ	ふ	ぐ	ラ	ロ	ハ	え	は	た	パ	ヌ	び	ち
デ	そ	レ	ぽ	ゆ	ン	フ	が	タ	ボ	ソ	え	つ	ノ	む
ザ	て	お	ゼ	モ	き	ん	レ	る	コ	ひ	の	き	ろ	ま
イ	た	や	ゆ	ン	お	ン	け	ン	リ	ソ	ガ	み	ヒ	お
ン	く	へ	マ	ス	ト	ぬ	エ	ノ	み	つ	ヨ	こ	い	か

Find the fifty words below in the square above, moving in a straight line in any direction including diagonals. The first thirty words are in *hiragana*, the rest *katakana*. (We found over two hundred other *hiragana* words, most of two symbols and not found elsewhere in this book. How many can you find? Fifty or more means you have a good vocabulary.)

* * * * *

madogiwazoku (staff passed over for promotion), *tsuridōgu* (fishing gear), *haragei* (nonverbal communication), *shitsurei* (rudeness), *kanji* (character), *fugu* (blowfish), *hinoki* (cypress), *kanemochi* (rich person), *ganbaru* (try your best), *daruma* (Buddha doll), *yuki* (snow), *tate* (verticality), *oya* (parent), *uchi* (home, inner group), *sewa* (care), *ongaeshi* (repayment of favor), *tsukimi* (moon viewing), *umeboshi* (pickled plum), *nemawashi* (behind-the-scenes maneuvering), *musubu* (bind), *nukeru* (be missing), *furusato* (hometown), *ame* (rain), *hosoi* (slender), *kaiko* (silkworm), *heta* (unskilled), *tanin* (stranger), *yoroi* (armor), *nama* (raw), *mizu* (water); *nairon, kiosuku, gurafu, dezain, terebi, hosuteru, warutsu, gasorin, furonto, puropera, purezento, kaunto, pasokon, misairu, tarento, rajio, gomu, masuto, denimu, yoga*. (Look up the *katakana* words you don't know.)

THE *IROHA* VERSE

The *iroha* verse was written about a thousand years ago. Though based upon a teaching of Buddhism its main use is for writing practice, for it includes all of the *kana* symbols with the exception of the final *n* (ん). In ancient times *mu* (む) was used where ん is used today. The order of symbols in the verse—particularly the first half dozen—is important because it is still sometimes followed in listings, in similar fashion to the English order "a, b, c."

Try copying out the verse in the space at the foot of the page.

いろはにほへど　　ちりぬるを
わがよたれぞ　　　つねならむ
うるのおくやま　　けふこえて
あさきゆめみじ　　ゑひもせず

The modern romanized version is: *Iro wa nioedo chirinuru o / Waga yo tare zo tsune naran / Ui no okuyama kyō koete / Asaki yume miji ei mo sezu.*

A literal paraphrase is: "Colors are fragrant, but they fade away. In this world of ours none lasts forever. Today cross the high mountain of life's illusions [i.e., rise above this physical world], and there will be no more shallow dreaming, no more drunkenness [i.e., there will be no more uneasiness, no more temptations]."

The above translation is given in the appendices of the *Japanese–English Character Dictionary* (edited by A. Nelson, published by Tuttle). Readers who wish to learn more about the historical use of *kana*, such as けふ for the modern きょう, are recommended to consult this work.

ANSWER KEY

Japanese Place Names Quiz (pages 106–107)
Cities 1. とうきょう 2. さっぽろ 3. せんだい 4. よこはま 5. なごや 6. おおさか 7. ひろしま 8. きょうと 9. ながさき 10. こうべ 11. ふくおか **Islands and prefectures** 1. ほんしゅう 2. ちばけん 3. きゅうしゅう 4. ほっかいどう 5. ぎふけん 6. しこく 7. さいたまけん 8. ひょうごけん 9. くまもとけん 10. かながわけん 11. おきなわ **Tourist attractions** 1. にっこう 2. にじょうじょう 3. びわこ 4. きよみずでら 5. きょうとごしょ 6. こうきょ 7. ふじさん 8. とうきょうスカイツリー 9. めいじじんぐう 10. おおさかじょう 11. せんそうじ

International Cities Quiz (pages 108–109)
1. Rome 2. Athens 3. Prague 4. Moscow 5. Sydney 6. Vienna 7. Baghdad 8. Jakarta 9. Santiago 10. Hollywood 11. Munich 12. Venice 13. London 14. Manila 15. Washington 16. Buenos Aires 17. Auckland (New Zealand) or Oakland (California) 18. Nairobi 19. Madrid 20. Kuala Lumpur 21. New York 22. Rio de Janeiro 23. Melbourne 24. Johannesburg 25. Cairo 26. Perth 27. Lima 28. San Francisco 29. New Delhi 30. Mumbai 31. Amsterdam 32. Kabul 33. Miami 34. Sao Paulo 35. Honolulu 36. Tel Aviv 37. Istanbul 38. Cape Town 39. Montreal 40. Paris 41. Berlin 42. Bangkok 43. Singapore 44. Lisbon 45. Oslo 46. Reykjavik 47. Addis Ababa 48. Manchester 49. Toronto 50. Chicago

Flora and Fauna Quiz (page 110)
1. いぬ 2. さかな 3. ライオン 4. たけ 5. かえで 6. ユーカリ 7. つばき 8. チューリップ 9. まぐろ 10. コアラ 11. にほんざる 12. カンガルー 13. ねずみ 14. あじさい 15. ハイビスカス 16. ひょう 17. カーネーッョン 18. かぶとむし 19. へび 20. ペンギン 21. ひらめ 22. ぼたん 23. マホガニー 24. すいせん 25. いちよう

Personal Names Quiz (page 111)
1. じろう 2. キャロル 3. れいこ 4. ノーマン 5. てるお 6. ウェンディー 7. まさよし 8. ヴァネサ 9. あけみ 10. ドワイト 11. けんいち 12. シェーン 13. ゆきこ 14. ジュリー 15. おりえ 16. ソフィ 17. つとむ 18. ウィリァム 19. ひでみ 20. ジャック 21. さわこ 22. デイビッド 21. のぞむ 22. エリザベス 23. ラッセル

Food Items Quiz (pages 112–113)
1. tempura 2. onigiri 3. ramen 4. karēraisu 5. yakisoba 6. tonkatsu 7. gyōza 8. edamame 9. umeboshi 10. misoshiro 11. takoyaki 12. tofu 13. omuretsu 14. shōyu 15. obentō 16. butaniku 17. gyūniku 18. toriniku 19. venison 20. sakana 21. maguro 22. tamago 23. yasai 24. kudamono 25. ringo 26. mikan 27. pan 28. chīzu 29. batā 30. hanbāgu 31. supageti 32. shichū 33. furaido

poteto 34. sarada 35. kashi 36. yōguruto 37. satō 38. bisuketto 39. pafe 40. aisukurīmu 41. purin 42. chokorēto 43. bīru 44. wain 45. nihonshu 46. jūsu 47. kōhī 48. remontī 49. kocha 50. ocha

Work and Play Quiz (page 114)

Occupations: せんせい teacher; かんごし nurse; がくせい student; いしゃ doctor; はいしゃ dentist; ウェブデザイナー web designer; べんごし lawyer; エンジニア engineer; けんちくか architect ; ウエーター waiter. **Pastimes:** やきゅうbaseball; どくしょ reading; ゴルフ golf; サーフィン surfing; テレビゲーム videogames; いけばな ikebana; バレーボール volleyball; カラオケ karaoke; じゅうどう judo; おりがみ origami.

Family Members Quiz (page 115)

1. はは 2. おかあさん 3. ちち 4. おとうさん 5. あね 6. おねえさん 7. いもうとさん 8. いもうと 9. あに 10. おにいさん 11. おとうと 12. おとうとさん 13. きょうだい 14. そふ 15. おじいさん 16. そぼ 17. おばあさん 18. つま 19. おくさん 20. おっと 21. ごしゅじん 22. かぞく

English version of "About Japan" (pages 116–117)

Let's look at an atlas. Japan is a long, thin country lying on a north-south axis to the east of the Asian mainland. It's about the same size as the state of California in America. It consists of four main islands. The largest is Honshu, with Tokyo at its midpoint. The beautiful Mount Fuji is also found on this island. The next largest is Hokkaido, the northernmost island. Summer here is cool, and in winter heavy snow makes skiing and skating possible. Kyushu, the third largest island, lies to the south, so it's warm here even in winter. The fourth largest, Shikoku, is noted for mikan oranges from its northern half and fish from the south.

English version of "Self-introduction" (pages 118–119)

I'm Sophie Smith. I live in Sydney, Australia. I'm studying Japanese at university. I live with my family in Sydney's famous Bondi Beach. There are five people in my family. My father is a dentist. My mother is a nurse. My older brother, David, works as a waiter in a seafood restaurant. My younger sister, Jane, is a high school student. My hobby is surfing. When I graduate from university I want to become a teacher of Japanese.

English version of "A Trip Abroad" (pages 120–121)

Last year I went to Japan for the first time. It was really wonderful. I was in Tokyo for three days. I went shopping in Harajuku, saw a traditional Japanese wedding at Meiji Shrine, and went up Japan's tallest building, the Tokyo Skytree. The weather was fine so from the Skytree I could see Mount Fuji. From Tokyo I went to Kyoto by bullet train. Kyoto's old temples are beautiful. My favorite temple was Kiyomizu. The food in Kyoto was delicious and I ate a lot of sushi.

PHOTOCOPIABLE